Original Intentions

Original Intentions

ON THE MAKING

AND RATIFICATION OF THE

UNITED STATES CONSTITUTION

M. E. BRADFORD

THE UNIVERSITY OF GEORGIA PRESS

ATHENS & LONDON

© 1993 by the University of Georgia Press
Athens, Georgia 30602
All rights reserved
Designed by Kathi L. Dailey
Set in Janson Text by Tseng Information Systems, Inc.
Printed and bound by Arcata Graphics
The paper in this book meets the guidelines for
permanence and durability of the Committee on
Production Guidelines for Book Longevity of the
Council on Library Resources.

Printed in the United States of America

97 96 95 94 93 C 5 4 3 2 1

Library of Congress Cataloging in Publication Data

Bradford, M. E. (Melvin E.), 1934–
    Original intentions : on the making and ratification of the United
States Constitution / M. E. Bradford.
        p. cm.
    Includes bibliographical references and index.
    ISBN 0-8203-1521-4 (alk. paper)
    1. United States — Constitutional history. I . Title.
KF4541.B68   1993
342.73′029 — dc20
[347.30229]   92-29851
                                                             CIP

British Library Cataloging in Publication Data available

For Marie, who makes it possible

CONTENTS

FOREWORD

In one of the marvelous essays you are about to read, M. E. Bradford writes that the argument he is making is not "a unique and personal achievement," and then he modestly adds, "though the way in which I support it may carry something of a signature." A signature, indeed! Though his writings can in part be categorized with general labels—he is a conservative, for instance, in the Burkean sense of the term, and he is a southern agrarian, in the Vanderbilt sense of the term—he is nonetheless a oner, if ever such existed. He is an English professor who has published a great deal of literary criticism but who more properly could be called a philosopher and more properly yet a prolific, provocative, and profound historian.

He describes himself as a rhetorician, which quietly and unintentionally suggests his uniqueness. What it does not convey, but what is evident on every page, is the almost awesome learning it entails in history, literature, and classical antiquity (sacred and profane), as well as the sensitivity to nuances in language and the literary skill that it requires.

As a rhetor—as such a rhetor—Bradford is singularly qualified to address the subject at hand. At issue here is the law, the organic law that is, or was, the Constitution of the United States: what he sets out to discover is what the American lawgivers had in contemplation when they established that instrument. Customarily, when scholars tackle that question, they turn to the records of the proceedings of the Great Convention that drafted the Constitution during the summer of 1787. But the fifty-five men who participated in the drafting were not, could not have been, the lawgivers, for they had no authority to make law. As was pointed out in the

convention by James Wilson (not Bradford's favorite Framer), the delegates were "at liberty to *propose any thing*," but were "authorized to *conclude
nothing*."

Those who did have the authority were the people of the several states,
acting separately through delegates to separate ratifying conventions. They
had the authority because the states were political societies which ante-
dated the existence of the United States and which had expressly reserved
their sovereignty when agreeing to the Articles of Confederation; and also
because to adopt the Constitution was to amend each of the state constitutions, and in the nature of things the people of one state could have no
power to change the constitution of another. For these reasons Bradford
has opted to follow the dictum of James Madison (likewise not his favorite
Framer) and to focus mainly upon the deliberations in the several states.

It has been said that the essence of creativity is to formulate a question,
a problem, or an investigation in a new way: that is what Bradford has done
here. Because the United States had not one body of lawgivers but thirteen,
and because the thirteen states had thirteen different histories, cultures,
heritages—sometimes widely different, as between New Englanders and
South Carolinians or between Rhode Islanders and other Yankees, sometimes subtly different, as between the denizens of Massachusetts and those
of Connecticut—it follows that what those lawgivers understood they were
doing varied from state to state. Hence Bradford's title: *Original Intentions*,
plural. All the states ratified the same Constitution, but each read it and
understood it in its own way.

In the hands of a less masterful rhetor, such an analysis might be caco-
phonic if not chaotic. In Bradford's hands it unfolds logically, orderly,
inexorably, beautifully, almost as if he were constructing a rose, petal
by petal.

Along the way, two related themes emerge. The first concerns the extremely limited ends for which the Constitution was designed and the extremely limited powers that it gave the partly national, partly federal government it authorized. Bradford quotes Roger Sherman and other Framers
on the subject, and I shan't duplicate those quotations here. Instead I offer
some anecdotal corroboration which, though he knows, he has not chosen
to cite, leaving me free to do so. On August 7, 1787, the Philadelphia Con-

vention was discussing the draft constitution reported the day before by the Committee of Detail, and an article setting the time and place for an annual session of Congress came up. Gouverneur Morris, an arch nationalist, moved to strike the clause, objecting to requiring a "meeting every year" on the ground that "the public business might not require it." Oliver Ellsworth, who was also ardent in his nationalism, said in rebuttal that "the Legislature will not know till they are met whether the public interest required their meeting or not." That rather graphically illustrates the Framers' understanding of how limited the national/federal government would be.

An incident in the career of Alexander Hamilton—who had a more activist approach to the use of the national government than perhaps any other American, or at least any other who obtained significant power—offers an even more striking example. In 1799, while commanding the American army during the quasi war with France, Hamilton wrote to Jonathan Dayton, Speaker of the House of Representatives, offering some suggestions as to ways the government could make itself stronger and more popular. One of these was the building of canals on inland waterways—what would come to be called internal improvements—at federal expense. But Hamilton, the great expositor of the doctrine of implied powers, thought that such canals could not be built unless a constitutional amendment to that end were adopted.

The second major theme running through *Original Intentions* is that of the tension between what Bradford (following Michael Oakeshott's formulation) calls nomocratic and teleological views of the Constitution. The nomocratic view, which accorded with the original understanding of almost everyone involved, is that the Constitution was designed to bring government under the rule of law, as opposed to achieving any specific purposes. That intention is evident to anyone who will take the trouble to read the document and do a bit of counting. Fully 20 percent of the text is specification of things that government, state or federal, may not do. Only 11 percent is concerned with positive grants of power. Most of the powers granted had already been vested in the old Confederation Congress, and of the ten new ones, all had previously been exercised by the states. Thus the sum total of powers that could now be legitimately exercised was diminished, not enlarged. The main body of the Constitution, more than two-thirds of it, addresses the task of making government act in accordance with law. To quote what I have written in another place — and to echo what Bradford says here and Oakeshott and Philip B. Kurland and others have said elsewhere — the Constitution "is primarily a structural and procedural document, specifying who is to exercise what powers and how. It is a body of law, designed to govern, not the people, but government itself; and it is written in language intelligible to all, that all might know whether it is being obeyed."

The alternative, teleocratic view is one that has come into fashion only during the last few decades and has all but destroyed the original Constitution. This is the notion that the design of the Constitution was to achieve a certain kind of society, one based upon abstract principles of natural rights or justice or equality or democracy or all of the above. It holds that the specific provisions of the document are of secondary importance or none at all; what counts are the "principles" it supposedly embodies, usually principles based upon the Declaration of Independence or Lincoln's Gettysburg Address, neither of which has any standing in law. The most effective advocate of the teleological view was Supreme Court Justice William J. Brennan, who, during the third of a century after his appointment in 1956, was arguably the most powerful — and, both Bradford and I would add, pernicious — figure in American government.

The last essay in this collection, which departs from the format but not the theme of the others, is necessitated by the ascendancy of the teleological school. Central to that school is the claim that the Reconstruction amendments (the Thirteenth, Fourteenth, and Fifteenth amendments, adopted during the aftermath of the Civil War) fundamentally altered the nature of the federal union, specifically through "incorporating" the Bill of Rights by making the first eight amendments apply to the states, as they had not done before, and more generally by substituting the second paragraph of the Declaration of Independence for the Constitution. Bradford subjects that claim to careful historical analysis and demonstrates that it is spurious: the original intentions of the framers of the Reconstruction amendments were moderate and in no sense aimed at effecting a constitutional revolution.

One final comment seems in order. Though the story of the perversion of the original Constitution is a sad and potentially tragic one, Bradford writes in hope, not in despair. His message, that of a quintessential southerner, can perhaps best be described by quoting the words of a quintessential Yankee, Daniel Webster: "Miracles do not cluster. Hold on to the Constitution of the United States of America and the Republic for which it stands—what has happened once in six thousand years may never happen again. Hold on to your Constitution, for if the American Constitution shall fail there will be anarchy throughout the world."

Forrest McDonald

PREFACE

This book is by nature and purpose an invocation of the patrimony. The eight chapters were written as part of the bicentennial observation honoring the Constitution of the United States. In particular, they salute the Constitution as it was when first drafted and ratified by the people of the states. Though these studies sometimes complain of contemporary misunderstandings in constitutional history, their informing principle is, obviously, my still undiminished regard for those who gave us our original form of government: both for the process which brought it into being and for the details of its design and operation as they affect us from day to day. The individual chapters were written first to be heard and then to be read— as the public statements of both scholar and citizen. For it is the nature of the American regime that an act of devotion to our constitutional morality, expressing our corporate will to "preserve, protect and defend" our Constitution, is ordinarily performed in speech of the kind the ancients called epideictic: not so much for debating policy or condemning error as for the rehearsal of attitudes generally agreed upon, necessary to the preservation of the nation's character and definitive of its special standing among the peoples of the world. Though long since distorted by construction and hidden beneath the encrusted details of a thousand ad hoc solutions to practical problems—solutions drawn up without a care as to their constitutional legitimacy—the old Republic of the Fathers is still there, visible within the misshapen effulgence of the United States Constitution as we presently experience it, waiting to have the barnacles cleaned away that, as amended, it may once more shine forth among the nations. Assuming the wisdom of this well-established American practice and the truth of these opinions concerning public piety toward a fundamental law that we treat as sovereign, that we use as a measure of all political legitimacy, these chapters have been left in the form in which they were prepared. For they are, first of all, addresses made in honor of a heritage, designed to argue a view of its content and to urge its preservation.

To be sure, many views of the enterprise under way were current among the Framers while they drafted and then, with great difficulty, agreed upon and helped to ratify the Constitution in their respective states. Furthermore, not all of these intentions could (or can) be reconciled with every alternative opinion as to what they were, collectively, attempting in the creation of a "supreme law of the land" — attempting even though they mostly agreed on the larger purposes of the Constitution and its "meaning" in the strict (operational or procedural) sense of the term. Max Farrand records from the notes of James McHenry of Maryland that on May 29, 1787, during the very first days of the Great Convention, Edmund Randolph, governor of Virginia, while introducing the so-called Virginia plan to his colleagues in Independence Hall, drew a contrast between the authors of the Articles of Confederation and the Framers of what he hoped would be the new United States Constitution. According to Randolph, the former company was made up of "wise and great men" whose study was "human rights" as that doctrine applied in their critique of the excesses of Great Britain. In other words, they sought to maximize rights of the sort violated by the Intolerable Acts by creating, in contrast to what came out of Whitehall, a minimal government, directly responsive at the local level to the population that it served. In the same spirit they had created the "democratic parts" of many state constitutions, especially concerning what the Fathers called "local police." As a result, "the powers of government exercised by the people swallowed up the other branches." Against such arrangements Randolph complained that "none . . . have provided sufficient checks against democracy." What the Framers were about to do would therefore not be about human rights or in behalf of democracy, except in a very limited way.

Randolph's preview of the intentions of the Framers represented the thinking of much of that company — perhaps of a small majority. But there were clearly other views of the business—of its structural impetus if not of its particular provisions. In Massachusetts, during the ratification convention held in Boston in January 1788, Fisher Ames announced a vision of government consonant with his Puritan heritage—a view that gave to his reading of the social implications of the Constitution a twist replicated only in the thinking of those Framers who found government to be the source of their liberty, not its adversary. He saw freedom outside the social condition as a Hobbesian chaos of untrammeled appetite and unruly passions such as had recently exploded in the western part of his state and in Vermont, New Hampshire, and Rhode Island. In behalf of the Constitution Ames conjured up the specter of Captain Shays and his desperate crew: "Anarchy and uncertainty attend our future state . . . who is there that really loves liberty, that will not tremble for its safety, if the federal government should be dissolved. Can liberty be safe without government? . . . The Union [preserved through ratification of the Constitution] is the dike to fence out the flood. . . . But when the inundation comes shall we stand on dry land?" The metaphor employed in this appeal explains what Connecticut Antifederalist Eliphalet Dyer meant when he reversed his position in his state's ratification convention and decided to support the Constitution as "a brave experiment to cope with the wickedness of mankind." Or what Ames himself intended when he observed, "Democracy is a volcano, which conceals the fiery materials of its own destruction." For Ames believed that men "cannot live without society," and that the people of Massachusetts should be (in John Winthrop's words) "knit together in this work as one body," made free and virtuous by their incorporation in the commonwealth and the Union. Energetic government as a fountain of blessings takes us back directly to the beginnings of the Protestant Zion in the Bay Colony. Other Framers, however, would have been uncomfortable with doctrines that were axiomatic for Fisher Ames.

For those who live inside the myth of an egalitarian America, it is perhaps surprising that so few of the Framers said anything about natural or equal rights during the course of the Great Convention, that Governor Randolph's opinion of their intentions as lawgivers was a sound one, vindicated after-the-fact of his prophecy by the records of those 1787 deliberations in Philadelphia. James Wilson of Pennsylvania was an exception to Randolph's prediction. Other Framers mentioned group rights, class rights, inherited rights, or property rights—the rights that go with membership in a society or specific rights earned by revolution, such as those a speaker sometimes invokes in the midst of a remark, though not to suggest serious philosophical generalizations concerning human nature. Furthermore, when in state ratification conventions or pamphlet literature certain Antifederalists assumed a strong position with reference to human rights, they were answered as was Major Samuel Nasson of Massachusetts—with the kind of deflating alternative explanation that John Rutledge offered in Philadelphia in response to too much lofty sentiment on the subject of slavery. With impatience toward idealists Rutledge had maintained that "interest alone is the governing principle with nations" and that only "fools" would proceed on another basis. In the same spirit Nathaniel Gorham of Massachusetts counseled his fellow lawgivers that they should "consult [the] rooted prejudices" of their constituents, and John Francis Mercer of Maryland insisted that all government was "by force and influence." It is a kind of evidence that none of the Framers were outraged by these recommendations for and constructions of the business at hand—that no one rose to refute them, that no one said nay to them. For all present agreed that they had been taught by experience "the danger of the levilling spirit"—the spirit which paid no attention to interests, prejudice, and influence. They were therefore also inclined to treat with suspicion lofty declarations of principle when they were employed as a prologue to self-serving propositions.

Of course, there were other theories as to the overarching purpose of the "more perfect Union" being proposed. These were either heard on the floor of Independence Hall, presented in the ratifying conventions, or developed in the literature of controversy that swirled around the Constitution once it had been delivered to the states. These theories went beyond simple questions of the conflict between rights and interests, either natural or not. The argument for the authority of experience, John Dickinson's "better guide than reason," was probably the most powerful of these doctrines. In all likelihood it was a predicate of Edmund Randolph's plan for a government based on something other than human rights. But the idea of a union for the sake of empire or the concept of government as an engine to promote wealth (positions advanced by Alexander Hamilton of New York and Oliver Ellsworth of Connecticut) could sometimes be connected with a view of the lessons of experience, a notion of group interests, an appeal to tested prejudice (like that praised by Edmund Burke), a plan for employing influence, or a set of assumptions about rights that are to be protected. Hence *Original Intentions*, the reference to many intentions, does not necessarily involve assumptions about irreconcilable differences. Instead, what it presumes is no more than a recognition of variety—though variety of a kind that made it necessary for the Framers to take great care in drawing up the compact which is our primary political bond. For if not all of these intentions can be served simultaneously, at least some of them can be reconciled to others some of the time, and with the nation retaining a coherence as both one and many. In attempting to perform such a task the Constitutional Convention followed one path and the ratifying conventions several others. This divergence has affected the historic development of the Constitution since 1789—both the legitimate amendments and the tendentious judicial or administrative readings of the text which have changed it without recourse to the Congress or the states.

Thus I have acknowledged multiplicity by distinguishing between various original intentions. However, though the contents of this book are eight speeches given on disparate occasions, it is by no means merely an after-the-fact collection. The subjects that these studies explore and the sequence in which they are assembled were predetermined before I began to work on the series and are assumed in what is said above about the word "intentions" as it functions in my title. The book had its name and purpose before it was written—even though, by happy accident, I was invited to deliver its several chapters as separate addresses during the celebratory years. Or rather, it assumed its final shape as I completed work on its central chapter, "Such a Government as the People Will Approve: The Great Convention as Comic Action," and asked where my analysis of the Constitutional Convention as dramatic structure might point with respect to the larger subject of the constitutional origins and development of the Republic. To the literary critic who is also a rhetorician, it is natural to focus on the dynamic of the various state ratification conventions. Moreover, because of my earlier work on the status of history as authority in the political deliberations of the Framers, I was predictably interested in assessing the role of eighteenth-century American attitudes toward the British constitution in shaping particular features of our Constitution.

Vociferous contemporary discussion of the standing of organized religion under the Constitution, combined with several years of work on brief political biographies of the Framers (both Framers in Philadelphia and Framers as leaders of ratification debates), inclined me to ask those synthetic questions that issued in "Religion and the Framers: The Biographical Evidence." Here, as in the essays on constitutional theory, political dynamics, and contrasting ratification conventions, certain general truths emerge—propositions concerning what can be believed about the lengths to which so many conventional but serious Christians would go in order to convert their country into a haven for unbelief, apostasy, or religious "neutrality"; generalizations about the unresolved variety of political motives that differentiate ratification in South Carolina or North Carolina from ratification in Massachusetts. And the same can be said about the Thirteenth, Fourteenth, and Fifteenth amendments, the so-called Reconstruction amendments, when their impact (with some associated legislation) on a Constitution originally procedural in nature—nomocratic and modest in its purposes—is defined. For it is what these amendments have come to mean that, under a heavy layer of melioristic *idées recues*, hides from us how little they in fact changed the nature of the minimal, limited federal instrument to which the Founders had agreed. Misconstruction of these amendments and laws has been the formula used to transform the Constitution of the United States into a purpose-oriented (that is, teleological) blank check for redesigning American society according to the advanced opinions of our savants. Correcting that misconstruction is therefore a necessary corollary to preserving or restoring the fundamental law. Hence my recourse to the theory of Michael Oakeshott in "Changed Only a Little: The Reconstruction Amendments and the Nomocratic Constitution of 1787" and my earlier comments on the relative importance of political doctrine and timing in "The Process of Ratification: A Study in Political Dynamics," a natural prologue to the readings of the several ratifying conventions.

The chapters of *Original Intentions* follow an order that, by increments, reinforces the argument of the book. In other words, their effect is accumulative. As I specify in the concluding essay on the amendments of 1865–70, the question addressed by the total set is not what lawyers and legislators, professors and judges as interested parties in the political struggles of this our era make of the document for their own objectives but what the authority is of the old Constitution itself, whose meaning (said Justice Sutherland) "is changeless" even though its "application is extensible": a Constitution that reproaches whoever would distort it to serve ends that are beyond its scope and subversive of its integrity. To that purpose it is most useful to search back before 1787 and to consider where the Framers' basic notions concerning the value of constitutions might have originated, and to recover especially their view of the British constitution — the eighteenth-century American reading of that political framework, one which brought England's North American colonies all the way into and through their Revolution. This task I attempt to perform in "The Best Constitution in Existence: The Influence of the British Example on the Framers of Our Fundamental Law." This essay looks back to the opening chapter on comic action and forward to my discussion of state ratifying conventions. According to the same interactive theory, it was necessary to speak of the Great Convention as a complete action before looking closely at one of its features — and to follow that segment of my analysis of the original Constitution with readings from two of the most distinctive state ratifying conventions in "A Dike to Fence Out the Flood: The Ratification of the Constitution in Massachusetts" and "Preserving the Birthright: The Intention of South Carolina in Adopting the United States Constitution." These papers, along with the later essay on ratification in North Carolina, "A Great Refusal: The North Carolina Ratification Convention of 1788," made way for emphasis on at least one of the now fashionable and well-established misreadings of those beginnings and of the "kind" of constitution Anglo-Americans only recently independent in 1787–88 could be expected to make. Only then could I begin to explain how the Constitution has come to so little resemble what the Framers expected it to be, even after two hundred years of national growth and development. I look back in the "Epilogue" at the almost inevitable consequences of ambition in a Supreme Court subject to no restraints apart from those that are self-imposed, called upon to restrict itself to a modest role when (obviously) all the rewards of power and fame will be offered only to such jurists as refuse any such confinement through fidelity to texts and instead invent the law.

Though I generalize from the information and analysis gathered in these pages, I try to confine my readings to certain themes and subjects within the range of my particular competence as a rhetorician. These studies point to others, and especially to a detailed examination of the assorted kinds of political rhetoric employed by eighteenth-century Americans. I focus here on the language and argument of American constitution-making because that subject has been especially neglected—the analysis of debates and of kinds of political persuasion that contributed to the finished work. But concerning the subject, I may summarize only from an overview of the various phases of the question seen as an order or chronological survey. That task I do attempt to carry out, despite the special character of my evidence. My hope is that this selection of subjects and texts confirms my argument with a reasonable economy, and without disguising or overlooking the complexity of the questions that it is bound to raise. The Constitution of the United States is a rich heritage of agreements elevated to the level of definitive act but without inflation into ideology and armed doctrine. It organizes and protects a government able to contain our multiplicity without setting out to resolve it. It does not manipulate our conflict over values toward some extrinsic, anterior goal. Rather, it tells us all that we are obliged to settle such questions *in society*, minus the coercions of law and politics. And that we should do so without those excesses of rancor that might pull down the entire edifice in impatience with its silence or reticence concerning many normative issues. The beginning of such restraint contains some understanding of the history of the United States Constitution, of how we have lost control of its interpretation, of how we may regain that control, and of why our fundamental law continues to be like Solon's, not the best we could invent but the best that the people would approve.

ACKNOWLEDGMENTS

"Such a Government as the People Will Approve: The Great Convention as Comic Action" was originally delivered to the students and faculty of the Southern Illinois University School of Law at Carbondale, Illinois, on February 26, 1987. It was first published in the *St. Louis University Public Law Review* 6 (Spring 1987): 215–28. "The Best Constitution in Existence: The Influence of the British Example on the Framers of Our Fundamental Law" was first delivered on October 20, 1987, at the University of Puget Sound School of Law in Tacoma, Washington. It was originally published in *Brigham Young University Studies* 27, no. 3 (Summer 1987): 51–66. "The Process of Ratification: A Study of Political Dynamics" was first delivered on November 16, 1989, before the Federalist Society at the Law School of Southern Methodist University in Dallas, Texas. It was published in *Chronicles* 15, no. 2 (February 1991): 18–20. "A Dike to Fence Out the Flood: The Ratification of the Constitution in Massachusetts" was, on April 22, 1987, presented before the Massachusetts Historical Society at Old Sturbridge Village, Massachusetts, and the following afternoon, at Dartmouth College in Hanover, New Hampshire. It was published in *Chronicles* 11, no. 12 (December 1987): 16–18, 20–23. "Preserving the Birthright: The Intention of South Carolina in Adopting the United States Constitution" was first given May 22, 1987, at the University of South Carolina Law Center in Columbia, South Carolina. Its initial publication was in the *South Carolina Historical Magazine* 89 (Spring 1988): 90–101. An abbreviated version of "A Great Refusal: The North Carolina Ratification Convention of 1788" came out originally in *Chronicles* 16, no. 7 (July

1992): 47–50. "Religion and the Framers: The Biographical Evidence" was published originally in *Benchmark* 4, no. 4 (1990): 349–58. It was first given as an address on November 13, 1990, in Lee Chapel at Washington and Lee University in Lexington, Virginia. "Changed Only a Little: The Reconstruction Amendments and the Nomocratic Constitution of 1787" was first prepared for the Claremont Institute for the Study of Statesmanship and Political Philosophy and was presented on February 13, 1987, on the campus of Claremont College in Claremont, California. It was then published by the *Wake Forest Law Review* 24, no. 3 (1989): 573–98.

For their assistance to me in the making of this book I wish to acknowledge the National Endowment for the Humanities, the Earhart Foundation, and the Marguerite Eyer Wilbur Foundation. In the preparation of first drafts of my essay on the three Reconstruction Amendments, I had also support from the Armstrong Foundation, known then as the Texas Educational Association, and the officers of Garvon, Inc.

I owe a special debt of gratitude to Cecelia Rodriguez, who typed the final version of the chapters, and to Debbie Winter, who did the copy editing of my manuscript for the University of Georgia Press. I must also indicate my appreciation of the advice, support, and encouragement I have received from the librarians of the University of Dallas, Jim McClellan, Ken Cribb, Eugene Meyer, Rennard Strickland, Tom Fleming, Jeff Hart, Clyde Wilson, Boyd Cathey, my son, Douglas, and my wife, Marie.

Forrest McDonald not only wrote the preface to this book but also read most of it in manuscript. Even so, he is not to blame for any of its shortcomings.

Original Intentions

1

Such a Government as the People Will Approve: The Great Convention as Comic Action

In our political system the fundamental law, the Constitution of the United States, is sovereign. Our public servants, both elected and appointed, swear their loyalty to it, as if to a prince, and undertake "to preserve, protect and defend" it against all enemies, foreign and domestic—a large order, to be executed only with care and caution. For as a prince may be distracted from his rightful function as father to his people by the blandishments of evil counselors, so may the fundamental law be drawn out of character by the strategies of interpretation and the interested manipulation of those who are responsible for its application. To understand and thus protect the Constitution is to know something of its origins, how it came into being and to what end. For those purposes (and in the spirit of bicentennial observation) this discussion focuses on the dramatic form and inceptional dynamic of the Great Convention and on the role of its protagonist, James Madison, in initiating, shaping, and then almost destroying the process of lawgiving that we especially associate with his name. I speak here as rhetorician, political and legal historian, literary critic, and old-time caucus politician. For all of these very different kinds of equipment (and more) are needed to tell the story which I have in mind.

The people who came together to draft the United States Constitution agreed on many things in advance. But nonetheless it was not at all certain that they would be able to produce a document that would result in the political reorganization of the United States—or indeed any document of any kind. Yet it made all the difference in how the business began and the course that it followed once under way that James Madison managed on May 29, 1787, to get his plan of government at the top of the agenda of the convention as the subject of its debates—and to get it there before any other plan was proposed.[1]

The human configuration Madison faced in the fifty-four other delegates from twelve states who, at one time or another, joined him in working toward the Constitution was full of unpredictable possibilities. In promoting his view of what the country needed to perfect the Union, Madison confronted a variety of opposing views, some completely obdurate and others more pliable. But other components of that assembly were either favorable to his plan of government or merely neutral. Whatever the business before the Great Convention, one would expect the loquacity of James Wilson (Pa.), Gouverneur Morris (Pa.), and Elbridge Gerry (Mass.) to be a part of the lawmaking achieved. Whatever Constitution might be proposed, Luther Martin (Md.), John Francis Mercer (Md.), Robert Yates (N.Y.), and John Lansing (N.Y.) would be against it. Moreover, the delegates of Delaware and New Jersey would insist on protection for their politically insignificant homelands, regardless of the other provisions of a new fundamental law. Led by William Paterson (N.J.) and the gifted John Dickinson, they would have their say. The Pennsylvania delegation, Alexander Hamilton (though sometimes indirectly), James McHenry (Md.), and Rufus King (Mass.) were resolved to help, wherever the struggle might lead. Benjamin Franklin acted to resolve tensions or conflicts. His presence was both iconic and "practical." And the considerable gentlemen from South Carolina and Connecticut were likely to have the swing vote in settling the disputes: John Rutledge, Pierce Butler, Charles Cotesworth Pinckney, Oliver Ellsworth, Roger Sherman, and William Samuel Johnson. South Carolina and Connecticut were determined not to give up and go home even after a protracted argument, but neither would they commit to any farfetched experiments.

Because he was not yet a major force in American politics or a prepossessing public figure, Madison chose the eloquent and youthful thirty-four-year-old governor of his state, Edmund Randolph, to present his (Madison's) handiwork to the convention in the form of fifteen resolutions. In order to get that assembly to move forward (and without committing themselves in specific to all of its parts) the other members of the Virginia delegation agreed to let it be understood that Randolph's proposals were not merely his own but Virginia's, which immediately gave them a larger importance than they would have enjoyed as one man's ideas. Of course, what facilitated the serious treatment received by Randolph's motions, once the Framers were resolved into a Committee of the Whole, was that General George Washington was in the chair when Randolph rose to offer them, was expecting those motions from that source, was, whatever the circumstances, going to recognize their advocate and treat him with respect since he (Washington) was already in support of the plan being recommended.

Randolph's big speech began with the traditional modest exordium in which he "expressed his regret that it should fall to him rather than those who were of longer standing in life and experience to open the great subject of their mission." He then mentioned the propriety of having a Virginian offer an opening motion because, by calling for the Annapolis Convention of 1786, Virginia had been responsible for the subsequent gathering of delegates in Philadelphia. Then came the surprise—not that Randolph should believe something so outrageous but that he should suggest it as a predicate for the deliberations that followed. For though most of the Framers came to the Constitutional Convention knowing that a piecemeal revision of the Articles of Confederation would not answer to their country's needs, they knew even better that a majority of the states would never have agreed to the meeting "had the idea of a total change" been mentioned as its probable consequence. Under these circumstances, no delegates would have been selected. Even so, Randolph made a circumstantial, historical argument against the existing Confederation as a system of government mindful only of "rights . . . clearly the chief knowledge of the times when it was framed," which is to say that the Articles came out of the special dynamic of the Revolution and were therefore filled with resentment of the abuses of government, so much so that they were indifferent to its legitimate claims against the citizen for support. Something more was now needed—more than "leveling" and the "excesses of democracy"—if peace, harmony, happiness, and liberty were to have any future in the United States. In large measure what Randolph suggested in his resolutions answered to the unstated agreement of the delegates present in the Constitutional Convention from the moment it convened, though a majority of these delegates also took exception to some part of his proposals.

The entire dynamic of the Great Convention follows from the fact that it begins with Washington in the chair and Edmund Randolph up to offer proposals. Those who have been part of a precinct, district, or state convention during a primary contest which is fought out in such a framework know that to get the gavel and then get your floor leader recognized for motions is to be better than two-thirds of the way toward victory. For to have a substantive motion accepted for discussion at the beginning of convention business puts it well on the way to getting it approved: is indeed, with the lukewarm and the indecisive, a way of legitimizing your list of candidates for delegates at large, your choice for delegation chairman, your preference in conflicts over credentials, and your list in the way of general resolutions for collective approval. What happened at the beginning of the Philadelphia Convention is that, in the phrasing of John P. Roche, "the framework of discussion was established on Madison's terms."[2] A motion given status by placement at the top of an agenda puts its opponents in a position where they must prove their case, not the other way around. It is therefore most interesting that the Virginia plan, despite all of its initial advantages, finally ran into trouble and became, in its eccentric provisions, more of an impediment to union than a guarantee for it.

The primary problem for the Madison/Randolph proposals was that, because they incorporated most of the a priori consensus of those who had accepted appointment as delegates to the proceedings in Philadelphia, and because their opponents acted reluctantly in opposing them (being pleased with most of what they contained), their advocates were misled into thinking of themselves as appointed "lawgivers," inventors of a new polity, free to reconstitute the social and political order of the United States. The truth of their situation, however, was that the Virginia Framers had no such implicit authority, free as they were to suggest anything they liked: that their proposals were, in certain particulars, so far from the consensus of their countrymen (to say nothing of their written mandate) as to threaten the hope of any common future under a fundamental law. They had misjudged the political situation of the unqualified nationalists who were only part of the political mix present in the Great Convention—the most outspoken and self-assured faction present there, but far from a majority—and in their arrogance and enthusiasm for government and all its works quite capable of alienating the delegates whose votes they needed if they were to overcome the reluctant and merely local-minded men who had sufficient strength to threaten the entire enterprise. The Virginians and their supporters failed to recognize that in a constitutional convention which would give the law to a people already very different from each other in countless ways, narrow majorities concerning the resolution of divisive questions were not enough to work with—not if they hoped to build a national unity that could survive popular upheavals, foreign invasions, economic tensions, cultural and regional differences, theological disagreements, and competing ambitions. But they could be expected to make this mistake before they were able to prescribe for the generations.

The other difficulty confronted by the proposals presented on behalf of Virginia is that, even in Virginia, they provoked those delegates who were unwilling to play lawgiver in advance of what other men might recommend to act that part in reaction—to take thought and specify, after the fact, what replacement for the Articles they could accept and still not be disloyal to the various identities they brought with them to the convention. These reactive or responding Framers tended not to be such thoroughgoing nationalists as those who approved almost immediately the items on the Madison/Randolph list. In other words, they behaved as conservatives often do—to their endless disadvantage in the context of modern politics. But since they did not reject most of what Madison had in mind, their reactions were delayed. Moreover, their final rigor in response to what they felt could not be endured was inconceivable to those who could imagine nothing worse than the "imbecility of government" without the power needed to collect a tax and defend a border. For they did not begin their thinking with the Revolution, did not attach priority to preserving "a degree of agency" for the states and some limit on the power of the remote and potentially hostile authority they were about to create in the place of King George III.[3] In this they differed both with the Antifederalists and with the cautious Framers, who were ready for a new government but fearful of "running into an extreme" of (in the language of Oliver Ellsworth) "razing the foundations of the building when they need only repair the roof."[4]

Those Framers who were forever advising Madison, Randolph, James Wilson, Gouverneur Morris, and Alexander Hamilton that the proper task of the Great Convention was to give the people "such a government" as they "will approve" (as opposed to the best they "could devise") were the men who, in the end, checked the impetus set in motion by the Virginia plan[5] and gave to the deliberations of the delegates another impetus, one that finally prevailed, resulting in the document with which we are familiar. As I have already suggested, the major difference between the various versions of the Constitution put forward in Philadelphia is that some of them leave a significant role for the states. It is with reference to his design for concentrating power in the hands of a general government that James Madison can be described as a classically comic figure and his experience in making and ratifying the Constitution a comic action. For what Madison almost caused was the breakup or dissolution of the convention that he had, in large part, brought into being. He was the occasion of a division among the Framers only one stage removed from adjournment—in the end depending on wiser men to repair the damage he had done.

According to Aristotle, the proper subject of comedy is ludicrous behavior, showing men not as better but as worse than they are,[6] at least until the moment of reversal, when they mend their ways and cease to move in the direction that has made them seem absurd. The classical definition of comedy in the *Poetics* is not fully developed and must be supplemented with illustrations from Greek drama itself and with modern commentary which develops the tradition if we are to understand how Madison's political experience in connection with the Constitution replicates the archetypal pattern of the genre to a remarkable degree. In comedy, reversal comes when those attitudes that have made for ridiculous contretemps are surrendered as a source of embarrassment and confusion, as in Aristophanes' *The Frogs*, where Dionysus, the patron of the Athenian drama, during a trip to the underworld changes his mind about which playwright he should bring back from death to inspirit a community in danger of losing its independence. After suffering a terrible but well-deserved humiliation that by an excess of cunning and cleverness he brought upon himself, Dionysus finally prefers the pious and prescriptive Aeschylus to the crafty Euripides, who is a subversive in his relationship to the accepted way. In *The Clouds*, an old farmer, Strepsiades, after being beaten by his own son, repents of having turned the boy over to the sophists to learn casuistry, dialectics, and how to avoid paying debts by arguing around the truth. Furious with himself for having trusted "chatterers" who "insulted the gods," the old man returns to his proper character by burning down the "reflectory" that is filling Attica with a foolish passion for ingenuity.

Northrop Frye, in speaking of the pattern of comedy, describes it as a "parabola": "a U-shaped plot, with the action sinking into deep and potentially tragic complications and then suddenly turning upward into a happy ending."[7] The bottom of this figure Frye calls "saturnalia," after the ritualized and socially purgative disorder of the Roman holiday—a moment when reality is inverted against its proper nature and turned upside down.[8] From his original mastery of the process of lawgiving, his situation as the guiding spirit, the intellectual ringmaster of the convention, Madison, in the course of his stubbornness in behalf of his plan, moves steadily downward toward a nadir, his peripeteia, in the moment when John Dickinson of Delaware upbraids him in exasperation, "You see the consequence of pushing things too far?"[9] The final turn comes on July 16 when the entire Constitutional Convention rejects his (Madison's) view on representation for the states. They adopt the report of the Compromise Committee elected on July 2—the suggestion of Benjamin Franklin. Eventually, the capacity for recognition of the situation comes and the resolution begins, moving away from the obsession, folly, forgetfulness, and pride that made it so difficult to achieve. But it does not come until there is a little more stubbornness, including appeals to savants who were more important to Madison as would-be lawgiver than that overwhelming majority of the people in a large majority of the states which he would need to get approval for any constitution drafted in Philadelphia. Because he was so attached to his view of the common good with respect to a fundamental law, so eager to "pursue a plan . . . which would be espoused and supported by the enlightened and impartial part of America" (that is, savants and philosophers, who can grant him fame), Madison had refused to recognize that there was any danger in insisting upon that view, regardless of what his colleagues might say.[10] "He was not apprehensive that the people of the small States would obstinately refuse to accede to a government founded on just principles"—principles he believed in.[11] And in this conviction he was utterly and inexcusably mistaken. Said another way, he was either self-deceived or else cared less for union than for the abstract purity of his plan, which is the attitude of the doctrinaire and the ideologue, not the statesman.

The three ingredients in the Virginia plan that gave it a divisive force were: (1) the membership from each state in both branches of the national legislature should be determined by population; (2) the national legislature should have a negative on laws enacted by the states; and (3) the national legislature should have power "to legislate in all cases to which the separate states are incompetent or in which the harmony of the United States may be interrupted by the exercise of individual legislation."[12] The last of these proposals is replaced in the Constitution by language speaking of a capacity "to make all laws which shall be necessary and proper for carrying into execution" aforementioned powers of the Congress and others "vested" in them by the explicit provisions of the Constitution. The replacement is a very different thing from what Randolph first proposed. Indeed, he was the first to retreat from that opening proposal on May 31, assuring Pierce Butler, John Rutledge, and other careful men that he had no "intention to give indefinite powers to the national legislature, declaring that he was entirely opposed to such an inroad on the state jurisdictions, and that he did not think any considerations whatever could ever change his determination."[13] Madison spoke in much the same way in Richmond on June 24, 1788: "Everything not granted, is reserved" (that is, to the states, or to the people). "Delegation [of an explicit variety] alone warrants the exercise of any power."[14] This is Jefferson's Madison—"self-evidently" a voice for the position reached by the Framers as a company—and not the young man who caused them all that trouble.

But it was the first two items on this list of mistakes and not the third that made it difficult for James Madison to retreat from the exposed position in which he was, for a time, either censured or ignored as a nuisance and resume his place as "almost" the father of the Constitution. The profound importance attached to the provision that the states be represented equally in at least one half of the Congress might naturally confuse recent immigrants such as Alexander Hamilton and James Wilson. For them the states were "imaginary beings." [15] But Madison should have heard and recognized the undercurrent of grumbling against his plan for reduction of the constituent members of the Union into hardly more than mere administrative districts: when Caleb Strong of Massachusetts spoke of the convention as being "nearly at an end"; when Roger Sherman observed "we are at full stop"; when Hugh Williamson predicted "our business must soon be concluded," with George Mason and William Richardson Davie in agreement; and when Benjamin Franklin suggested public prayer. [16] He should have listened and retreated from such tremors of the earth in recognition of real power over his ambitions and designs—the hobbyhorse that he rode toward fame, until "unseated" in the fierce debate over representation. That he was listening to other music instead of the baleful iteration of these predictions of adjournment *sine die* can be demonstrated by his functional indifference to the structure of the Great Convention itself. For he failed to treat it as an assembly representing the people of the states— failed to recognize that, as William Samuel Johnson argued, "the states do exist as political societies," not just as pieces of geography, and "must be armed with some power of self-defence." [17] Because they had for raw material subject to their shaping hands a going, functional, social, economic, and political order instead of some philosophical *tabula rasa*, the eventually successful Framers worked outward from that given reality. They assumed responsibility for the preservation of that order: a structure in which the states were the most important ingredients of continuity, elements that defined what kind of polity Americans would accept as a legitimate consequence of their Revolution. Therefore the political theory built into the original American regime is a doctrine that structurally informs the very sequence by which they arrived at the Constitution "as it was"—a theory embodied in the process by which the Constitution was ratified, and the method still employed when it is revised by amendment.

Concerning the power to negative legislation passed by the states, Madison gave way much more readily than on the subject of representation. Perhaps he did so because that provision of the Virginia plan was rejected after the Great Compromise had been adopted by the convention—in that Madison was already a defeated lawgiver, with less of his vanity at stake in an idea he never fully expected to pass into law. However, although the issue of the negative brought with it no danger of an adjournment, and came to a vote during the resolution of Madison's comic drama, I believe we make a mistake if we take lightly either his ideal or his support of it. For he continued to recommend it long after the subject was closed, stubbornly exasperating his colleagues as late as August 28, 1787.[18] Gouverneur Morris called the power in question "terrible to the states" and predicted it might "disgust" its opponents.[19] John Lansing of New York described it as potentially even "more injurious" than the British government's negative over the American colonial legislatures.[20] Roger Sherman insisted that the power they were creating should be forbidden "to interfere with the government of the individual states in any matters of local police."[21] Williamson inveighed "against a power that might restrain the states from regulating their internal police."[22] Luther Martin, John Dickinson, and George Mason spoke of the danger of leaving too little political capacity in the states, means insufficient to foster consensus in working its way upward from local communities, reflecting the "genius of the people,"[23] which was also the expressed opinion of the New Jersey delegation, the Pennsylvania delegation, Pierce Butler, and Elbridge Gerry.[24] In announcing his "fear" that they were "running into an extreme in taking away the powers of the states," Butler spoke the good sense of the Great Convention as a whole, as rendered unmistakably on July 17, 1787, by a vote of seven states to three—a wisdom that gave the final drafting of the Constitution into hands other than those of James Madison, to a committee chaired by the absolutely conservative John Rutledge of South Carolina. In the end, the would-be lawgiver was obliged to accept the handiwork of other men as "the law of the land," voting on the losing side on more than half of the recorded divisions in which he took part.

In response to the ambitious notions of Madison and his friends, their plans for re-creating America, the judicious Roger Sherman suggested a set of purposes to be served by whatever constitution he and his more temperate associates might produce. The objects of union he believed were few: (1) defense against foreign danger; (2) control of internal disputes and disorders; (3) treaties; (4) foreign commerce, and a revenue to be derived from it.[25] Though in September 1787 he gave it only grudging approval, it is a great irony that, in fully completing the comic pattern here under examination, in 1788, in Richmond, James Madison defended the Constitution he had attempted to prevent: defended it as a minimal instrument—more or less what Roger Sherman had in mind. It was Madison's argument in the Virginia ratification convention (and later, as Democratic-Republican leader in Congress), his reading of the Preamble, that the Constitution was no more than what a very moderate Federalist should accept: that "the powers in the general government are those which will be exercised mostly in time of war," that they by and large "relate to external objects" and represent no real change from the Articles of Confederation except in providing a machinery for enforcing tax laws and a few other regulations agreed upon before the Framers met in Philadelphia.[26] In other words, he says, shading away from his position in *The Federalist*, that the Constitution does not create a national government, that it means, where it is silent, that what it does not authorize explicitly it will not allow: that "by enumerating [certain rights] of government it implied there were no more." Such a government would have been almost modest enough in its capacities to suit the Antifederalists had they completely believed what Madison said.[27] These doubts aside, however, the spectacle of Madison in the Richmond Convention brings us to that moment when erstwhile enemies are at least formally reconciled, a moment that Aristotle tells us to look for at the end of a comic action—a point that is not only ironic but hopeful. For in Richmond Madison was (despite his difficulties there) finally the lawgiver—one with Benjamin Franklin, John Rutledge, Roger Sherman, Oliver Ellsworth, John Dickinson, Pierce Butler, Hugh Williamson, William Samuel Johnson, and the other moderate men who worked with them to give the people such a government as they would approve—regardless of how far short of theoretical perfection it might fall.

The most important teaching to be abstracted from close examination of the events described in these remarks is that there is no place in a healthy political atmosphere for domination by the *idée fixe*—a warning against system, ideology, and abstraction, even of a modest sort. The making of the Constitution was a limited, political, non-philosophical act, reflecting a consensus about the nation's future hopes and present character, performed by men whose agreements with one another grew in the process of hammering out certain differences of opinion about the common good in relation to the particular good of their own communities. They came to understand out of their experience under the Articles that, given the already established fact of American multiplicity and the well-founded suspicion among their neighbors regarding remote and arbitrary authorities, very large majorities would be necessary to establish a fundamental law: or, reflecting their wisdom and foresight concerning those of us who inherit two hundred years later, necessary to change it by amendment. Because the Framers knew the value of such majorities they also knew how to make them—both in Philadelphia and through the state ratifying conventions. They made compromises over what other men thought to be matters of principle, thus following the advice of Plutarch's Solon which they were so fond of repeating: advice about the danger of attempting to create the best government they could imagine.[28]

Another lesson carried by all of this evidence is that, contra the partisan and insupportable obscurantism of Justice Brennan, what the Framers intended by the Constitution, especially in the political equivalent of "matters of faith and doctrine," can be ascertained and applied to the most familiar modern misunderstandings of its provisions. The purpose of our form of government is embodied in the procedures for dealing with one another politically that are its primary regulations. It is true that the Constitution presupposes the Declaration of Independence and also the Articles of Confederation, but only in a restricted sense, within the limits of the powers it creates. The Constitution establishes a regime both federal and national, replacing a confederation that it revises and contains, based on the achievement of the independence merely declared in 1776. But it is not an instrumental, substantive document drawn up to foster the favorite capital-letter abstractions of the millenarians. It is more concerned with what government will not do for each of us than with the positive description of acceptable conduct, which is left to local and idiosyncratic definition—to society, local customs, and tested ways.[29] Most important, it is not about enforcing the abstract "rights of man" or some theory of perfect justice and aboriginal equality, not even with the Bill of Rights added to it. For at least until the June 1866 passage by Congress of the Fourteenth Amendment, these guarantees did not apply to the states. (Here we leave aside the still unsettled question of what that amendment really meant.) In the Constitution proper (as in the discussions that shaped it) there is almost no mention of any species of equality: not even of the equality of citizens before the law. Instead, with respect to individuals, the Constitution promises the advantages of living under a particular republican political system, a representative government, elected fairly according to certain established procedures, providing against the danger of tyranny with a calculated division of powers among the three branches of the federal structure, a reservation of powers to the states, and a limit of law on what may be attempted by any or all of these components vis-à-vis the private lives of individual citizens. It provided for these rights and also a few others, which are specified so as to secure that republican political system against offenses which the Framers thought might very well pull it apart.

Hence we understand the provisions for the sanctity of contracts, for trial by jury (in criminal cases), and against state and local influence over the process of immigration; the regulation of interstate commerce—necessary, given the powers left with the states; the language precluding foreign grants, titles, and social distinctions (obnoxious as sources of unearned status); and the guarantee of a "Republican form of government." And to this list we may attach a heterogeneous assortment of other provisions that authorize or forbid particular policies with respect to particular citizens: the rules governing the transfer of "privileges and immunities" from one state to another; the prohibition of bills of attainder and ex post facto laws; protections for patents and copyright; the securities given slaveowners and the holders of indentures against runaways and those who would encourage them; the safeguards for writs of habeas corpus; and the assurance that criminals will not escape punishment by flight across state lines. These rights are included and a few more, but not many.

Instead, the larger pattern of intent to be inferred both from what the Constitution says and what it does not say is that it leaves much of the relationship between Americans to be worked out by "private treaty." The implications are clear. The meaning of civic virtue, of citizenship, is, under these terms or arrangements, one that wells up from the source, from the "genius of the people," not the a priori dialectics of the philosophe or projector. In other words, it is not "provided" by the Constitution. Apart from "the blessings of liberty," the promise of the Preamble is fulfilled by leaving questions of value to be settled by something other than the federal power. Or at least this is what the Framers expected, aiming, as Forrest McDonald has well said, at "government of the sort to which they were accustomed" in all but a few external matters.[30]

Most Federalists, as much as the local-minded Antifederalists, recognized the impropriety of making the Constitution of the United States into a security for the rights of citizens in their own states or communities. Even so strong a centralizer as Theodore Sedgwick of Massachusetts, later Federalist Speaker of the House of Representatives, realized that the more guarantees of personal rights are included in the fundamental law, the less freedom Americans can hope to enjoy. As he wrote a friend during the struggle over ratification, "had the national government undertaken to guaranty the several rights of citizenship in their [the states'] declaratory bills, it would have been given a right of interference which would naturally tend to check, circumscribe and finally annihilate all state powers."[31] And the entire Congress of the United States spoke to the same effect when, during the First Congress, the House of Representatives refused to allow James Madison to apply even a few provisions of the Bill of Rights as restrictions upon the states.[32] Their action recalls the anger of Patrick Henry in the Virginia ratifying convention when Governor Randolph spoke anxiously of the case of the Virginia bushwhacker Josiah Philips, who had been caught and hanged, as an instance of irregularity such as would be prevented by the Constitution. The legislature of their state had approved of this summary execution without trial—in Randolph's view, an instance of ex post facto law. Henry's response was that the people of Virginia knew what they were doing, and, unlike "modern statesmen," had no "illuminated ideas" or "imagination" to make them worry about such incidents since they did not reason concerning government on the basis of abstract "political speculation."[33] Edmund Randolph had made a mistake in bringing the matter up. Other Federalists steered the debate away from the case of Josiah Philips, for Federal supervision in questions of "local police" meant that the Constitution had a substantive character and might be applied to the reformation of our local habits and attitudes. That was not the kind of suggestion calculated to overcome the eloquence of Patrick Henry or to confound the Antifederalist leadership in other states. To the contrary, an emphasis on restraining disorders could be expected to cost the Constitution much support. For that reason James Madison emphasized its largely external objectives and said nothing about due process, substantive or otherwise. Such a doctrine would have defeated the Constitution, so foreign was it to the vision of the Framers.

Finally, we should be convinced by the structure of the Great Convention as a dramatic action and by its aftermath in the rest of his political career that even more than Madison in his designing of a government or in his role as advocate for his plan in the Constitutional Convention or in *The Federalist* we should pay our particular respects to James Madison as he first appeared in the Virginia ratification convention. For, speaking here of stages in his development, the distance between that Madison and his Antifederalist opponents was not so great as to obstruct the establishment of a government or to make of that establishment a political threat to the inherited way of American life as it already existed. Moreover, what Madison says at this point is a close approximation of the convictions of his countrymen at large, closer even than what he gives us as Publius in that he argues finally for a Constitution that "the people will approve." As he himself declares, "the meaning of the Constitution is to be sought . . . not in the proceedings of the body that proposed it, but in those of the state conventions which gave it all the validity and authority it possesses." He then adds, "if the sense in which the Constitution was accepted and ratified by the Nation . . . be not the guide in expounding it, there can be no security for . . . a faithful exercise of its powers."[34] In some of the ratifying conventions we might also find that Constitution, hidden from us in our day by the "inventions and concoctions" of judicial distortion but subject to recovery even now. Only by honoring that Constitution (as opposed to its lesser, "modern" antitypes) do we act in the spirit of bicentennial observation, struggling as did its Framers to "secure the blessings of liberty" to the succeeding generations.

2

The Best Constitution in Existence:
The Influence of the British Example
on the Framers of Our Fundamental Law

When in 1787 a carefully chosen body of distinguished citizens from twelve of the original British colonies in North America met to consider how they should go about improving or replacing their existing bond of "perpetual union" in the Articles of Confederation, they enjoyed as a basis for their deliberations an agreement on what they meant by a constitution: a "fundamental law." Both for the outlines and for the details of that concept they went primarily to the example they knew best: to the history of the English constitution in whose name they had recently achieved an independence ironically outside of the protections of that authority. Contrary to what Sir Henry Maine observes in his *Popular Government*, the Constitution of the United States is not "a modified version of the British Constitution which was in existence between 1760 and 1787."[1] For its prototype is the minimal constitution put aside with the passage of the Stamp Act, the constitution of 1688 that was a bond by way of inheritance, shaped more by corporate memory than by first principles: a legal bond, composed of a few texts, favored glosses upon these texts, and a disposition or habit of mind most easily identified with the Whig magnates of eighteenth-century England—magnates whose speakers put text, gloss, and memory together.

Because it is the current fashion to read history backward, tracing the records of actions and attitudes retrospectively from our time through 1763 instead of forward from, shall we say, the Norman Conquest, it is predictable that this generation should persist in construing the United States Constitution in a vacuum, that they should forget how most of our American forebears cherished the English constitution and did not change their opinion of its merits just because Parliament and the ministers of King George III failed to observe some of its provisions. When we see the Framers in proper historical context, it becomes clear that their handiwork, like its prototype, "was the result not merely of philosophy, but of an historical upgrowth."[2] Sir Herbert Butterfield, in noting the difference between the political spirit of Western man since the French Revolution and how he had once, long before 1789, responded to the intractable difficulties of human coexistence and social order, has remarked that men "make gods now, not out of wood and stone, which though a waste of time is a fairly innocent proceeding, but out of their abstract nouns, which are the most treacherous and explosive things in the world."[3] Because they came out of the American version of the English experience still admiring the non-ideological British constitution, because (in most cases) they pled no larger arguments for revolution than the law, and at worst spoke of no authority beyond its text (saving only the right of self-preservation), the members of the Great Convention divinized no abstractions, avoiding with conscious intent the now familiar language of multitudinous "rights" and thus the idolatry of which Butterfield has written.

In an era that urges us from every quarter to accept the notion of the United States Constitution as a bundle of general propositions about the a priori purpose of government and its function in fulfilling the expectations generated by a universal human nature, in an age that recognizes in the fundamental sovereign law little more than a set of anterior programmatic, social, economic, and political goals to be achieved by inventive constructions of the silences of the Framers, which sees only problems in the limitations placed upon its scope by its very nature, it is difficult to overemphasize the English constitutional inheritance of the American people. For, as its enemies obliquely proclaim in noisy denials of its importance, a public memory of that inheritance has heretofore stood almost alone in the way of certain kinds of chaos. It is a memory that precludes mischief already in motion and other mischief (judicial and legislative) soon to be attempted in the name of "constitutional principles"—misnomers extrapolated from the "sacred text" by people who know next to nothing about its origins and have no intention of correcting what they find to be, for their own purposes, a useful ignorance.

The Whig legalists who authored and then ratified the American Constitution did not, however, proceed at so great a remove from the spirit of modernity out of ancestral piety or by reason of the British constitution's overall impact on their lives (though it had been clearly beneficent). Instead, they were moved to emulation by its specific virtues that they had come to value more and more as they fought to protect them during the Revolution and then struggled to institutionalize them as part of American law once the fighting had ended. Perpetuation was their objective, even sometimes when they modified the British original—as in making their Constitution entirely a thing written down.

It has been argued that as much as three-fourths of the document approved by the several states (including the Bill of Rights) makes no sense apart from an intimate familiarity with British legal history. Studies of our Constitution written before 1930 emphasized these continuities.[4] I will in passing mention only a few.[5]

From the English Bill of Rights we derive our guarantees of regular sessions of Congress, our rules prescribing that money bills originate in the House of Representatives, our protections for the privileges of Congress to regulate itself, many limitations on the President's power, and the elaborate provisions for the impeachment of government officers of every description, including federal judges. The language in our Constitution protecting the writ of habeas corpus comes from the English Act of 1679 treating of that subject (31 Chas. 2, c. 2, 27), and before that from the Magna Carta (31 Car. 11, 6.7, 8). The English Bill of Rights is also reflected in the First, Second, Fifth, Sixth, and Eighth amendments to the United States Constitution. The First and Third amendments also derive from 3 Chas. 1, c.l, 7, June 1628—the glorious Petition of Right, which King Charles I made law by giving his assent to it while sitting in the midst of his Parliament. The definition of treason is of course from

Edward III's 1352 Statute of Treasons—and a protection of the subject against political prosecutions. For protection of the right to petition and assemble and of the particular right not to be amerced except from a judgment of one's peers, according to the law of the land, the source is antiquity itself, the Great Charter—especially chapter 39 in the original text signed by King John, where it is required that "no man be taken or imprisoned but *per legem terrae*, that is, by Common Law, Statute Law or Custome of England. . . . No man shall be disseised . . . unless it be by the lawfull judgement, that is, verdict of his equals, (that is men of his own condition) or by the Law of the Land (that is to speak it once for all) by the due course and processe of Law."[6] Thus originates the most widely accepted rendering of our most fundamental guarantees of the liberties (as opposed to liberty) of the subject, from Sir Edward Coke's *The Second Part of the Institutes of the Laws of England*. Behind this paraphrase is the Latin of 1215.

Nullus liber homo capiatur, vel imprisonetur, aut disseisatur, aut utlagetur, aut exuletur, aut aliquo modo distruatur, nec super eum ibimus, nec super eum mittemus, nisi per legale iudicium parium suorum vel per legem terre.[7]

Attached to Coke's rendering of the essential passage are others linking the king's majesty and the necessities of the royal purse with the orderly processes through which a free people tax themselves. Finally, in the matter of the authority of the law over the will of princes and parliaments, the ground for even thinking of a constitution as possible, there are the Jacobean digests that, together, presuppose a sovereign law, that, in the language of Bonham's case (8 Co. Rep. 107a, 114a [CP 1610]), we are assured with respect to any positive law or judgment "against common right and reason [that] . . . the common law will control it and adjudge such act to be void." Inside this matrix of promulgations, charters, customs, cases, and prescriptions emerge most of the particular properties, features, and provisions of the United States Constitution that do not have to do with the shortcomings of the Articles of Confederation, certain specific problems of the newly independent nation, republicanism or federalism. And even the latter had its origins in the operations of the British constitution among Englishmen in North America, as had, according to Madison, the idea of judicial review as a way of preserving the Constitution whenever threatened, a procedure inspired by the examination given to the acts of American legislatures and governors by the Board of Trade or the ministry in power. To approach the text of the Framers' Constitution without knowing the history of the Norman Conquest, the War of the Roses, the attainder of the Earl of Strafford, or the Glorious Revolution, to read it without some introduction to the English Civil War of the 1640s and the eighteenth-century debate about the nature of rightful authority over free Englishmen is to misconceive the purpose embodied in the new American Constitution as it stood in 1791 — especially where the document embodies improvements in its model and prototype that British statesmen had been proposing for generations: privileges and immunities, proscriptions of de post facto laws, bills of attainder, Star Chamber proceedings, and the like.

What unites this partial survey of connections and derivations is precisely that they concern primarily discrete, particular commitments, not generalized positions. Contained in these guarantees is no equal protection or general welfare or necessary and proper fanfaronade; yet the commitments are most valuable because they are not subject to distortion by construction and extrapolation into whatever judges or legislatures, for extra-constitutional reasons, might make of them. But the most important of these established reasons for the Framers' honoring and valuing the inherited constitution made over time by their ancestors was its protection of the political liberty of subjects, the freeholders, in the exercise of their customary, inherited, and chartered rights of self-government. The hope of the members of the Philadelphia Convention of 1787 was to frame a document that would do the same for themselves and for succeeding generations of Americans.

Consideration of the impact of the British constitution on the workings of the Great Convention should not begin with the subject proper but with the one hundred and fifty years of the colonial history of British North America as an extension and completion of an antecedent English identity. Americans, we must remember, had a long and unbroken experience of adopting a British original to their peculiar purposes before they undertook to replace the prototype with a unifying, homemade substitute. As no less a judge than Edmund Burke maintained, the original United

States Constitution has the virtue of being a version of the British constitution "well adapted to its circumstances." By preserving what was useful from the inherited structure of English government as it stood in 1787, by utilizing the "republican education" achieved in the process of governing themselves in colonial British America, the Framers authored a revision of the total system that connected them as countrymen. It is a revision that has the merit of not attempting to "conquer absolute and speculative liberty," being satisfied with a lesser and more durable ambition.[8] That lesson English citizens had learned before they reached these shores. They relearned it thoroughly in governing themselves in all but a few respects as overseas subjects of the Crown in the New World under various royal charters. Led by both appointed and elected chief magistrates, Americans enjoyed a version of self-government that provided for no taxes but such as they put upon themselves. The lack of a resident nobility and a complete religious establishment, along with the remoteness of the king and his imperial machinery, made them a different sort of English subject. But not too different! For even three thousand miles from Lands End, the British constitution was their context for thinking about politics—a constitution already (according to John Adams) "republican," but given an even more republican flavor by distance, diminution, and distinctions of circumstance in the New World.

English colonials in North America, as has been demonstrated in recent scholarship, developed a great interest in constitutional questions during the Glorious Revolution and took sides in the significant disputes about the relation of prince to fundamental law within the larger English tradition.[9] They preserved their place within the patrimony of an inherited political system by transplanting and applying the common law of England to their own unique situations and by deriving, theoretically, the legitimacy of their own local systems of government from their origins in the acts of the Crown in Parliament or the antecedent exercises of unquestioned royal prerogatives. Their laws were the outworks of a general constitution, provisions of which applied only to them. Other components made outside the mother country might be applicable only to Scots or Canadians or the Irish—with the ancient constitution itself resting underneath them, linking into oneness all such local variety. In the days of the Stamp Act

Crisis, during 1765–66, all freemen on this side of the Atlantic invoked the quintessentially English idea of a sovereign law that personified the national character by being derivative of the entire national experience: the law of Henry de Bracton that both makes and unmakes princes, a power "superior" to the king, "through which he has been made king."[10] All of the British colonies in North America invoked the constitution against Parliament in its unsanctioned claims of supremacy. They insisted that Parliament could not vote as it wished if in violation of fundamental law. If the constitution were to be strictly observed by all who had authority, Americans had nothing to fear. So said John Dickinson and Daniel Dulany and other protesting pamphleteers. Their professed loyalty was to a legal inheritance and to the institutions designed to give it force — incidentally, conditionally, according to the cases: so long as those institutions served the ends for which they were supposedly created. The British constitution meant mixed government and a separation of powers, with a local legislature for all local issues: a little Parliament with courts attached, supported by American taxes. Therefore it meant a check upon despotism, which everyone deplored as a condition to be avoided, the antithesis of rule of law. The Crown would sometimes be represented by governors, sometimes by the Board of Trade or various ministers. The King's Bench (his judges) either enforced the constitution or forfeited their authority. Out of these adaptations emerged a fully developed notion of a fundamental law, logically prior to the assertion of legislative supremacy or the royal prerogative or even abstract principle. In arguing against the Sugar Act, the Stamp Act, and subsequent assertions of a remote, hostile, and arbitrary power, Americans prepared themselves to envision a particular constitution of their own, a fundamental law that would preclude such errors; and also they developed an idea of what it would be like to observe such a law.

While it shaped their side of the argument with Whitehall and George III's ministers, propelling them toward pressing that case to its logical conclusion in an assertion of the right of independent self-preservation within the British constitution as it stood after the abdication of James II (minus monarch, and much else besides), the version of this constitution preserved among its American apologists also acted as a check on how much their "struggle" might attempt or signify in the way of radical change in the local operations of their laws, their economic political systems, and the rest of their culture. A revolution on these grounds could be revolutionary only up to a point; and once independence had been formalized in the September 1783 Treaty of Paris, the same reverence for the English constitutional achievement surrounded, conditioned, and provided a language for reflection on their own legal necessities. Of course, there were radicals at the fringe of the American body politic—even a few close to the center—and a number who would have been pleased to believe with Patrick Henry (though for very different reasons) that what distinguished the new American government was that it had "not an English feature in it."[11] But among those capable of coherent, consistent political thought (as opposed to mere protest) there were not many radicals, and those few who did enjoy a temporary influence worried other Patriots to no end since the characteristic concern regarding constitutions had to do with setting limits on change.

As a sample of the operation of these restraints, we should consider the 1774 speech of James Duane of New York, president of the Continental Congress, which recommended, as opposed to some teaching on natural equality, "grounding our Rights on the Laws and Constitution of the Country from whence we sprung."[12] Or, for an equivalent to Duane's Old Whiggery, we might examine the eloquence of Carter Braxton of Virginia, who in May 1776 urged independence upon the citizens of the Old Dominion from the example of 1688—but *no more than independence*:

> The testimony of the learned Montesquieu is very respectable. "There is" (says he) "one nation in the world, that has for the direct end of its constitution political liberty. . . ."
>
> This constitution and these laws have also been those of Virginia, and let it be remembered that under them she flourished and was happy. The same principles which led the English to greatness, animates us. To that principle our laws, our customs, and our manners are adapted, and it would be perverting all order, to oblige us, by a novel government, to give up our laws, our customs, and our manners.
>
> However necessary it may be to shake off the authority of arbitrary British dictators, we ought nevertheless to adopt and perfect that sys-

tem, which England has suffered to be so grossly abused, and the experience of ages has taught us to venerate. . . .[13]

John Jay of New York, at this stage in his career, sounds very like his ally from Virginia. First he objects to any rush toward independence because he doubts that "all government is at an end" — that George III and his ministers have broken all bonds between Great Britain and its colonies on these shores as James II forfeited his royal authority in the mother country almost ninety years earlier. Before the Continental Congress he declares, "The measure of arbitrary powers is not yet full and I think it must run over before we attempt to frame a new Constitution."[14] Later, when that measure had been accomplished, Jay went forward to a secession "in defense of old liberties, not in search of new."[15] Thus, looking back in 1800, he describes not only himself but the entire Continental Congress from 1774 to 1776. In letters of the time he often invokes the law of self-preservation.[16] And in his October 1775 "Address to the People of Great Britain," Jay appeals to the sanction of inherited rights, following the pattern of other well-respected Whig resistance to tyranny.

Further examples of piety toward English institutions among a people at war with Great Britain are preserved in John Drayton's *Memoirs of the American Revolution from Its Commencement to the Year 1776.* The "Address to His Excellency, the Right Honorable Lord William Campbell" on June 25, 1775, from the Provincial Congress of South Carolina was probably written by John Drayton's father, William Henry Drayton, the principal theorist of the Revolution, for his very conservative community. Yet what Drayton says here is echoed at other times by John Rutledge, Henry Laurens, Charles C. Pinckney, Edward Rutledge, and Rawlins Lowndes: that Carolinians have, even as they stand ready to fight, "no love of innovation — no desire of altering the Constitution of Government — no lust of independence"; that "Carolinians wish for nothing more ardently than a speedy reconciliation with our mother country, upon constitutional principles"; that Carolinians love the British constitution, even in "taking up arms" as the "result of dire necessity, and in compliance with the first law of nature."[17]

It is a simple matter to find the same kind of Whig doctrine coming from leading figures in each of the original thirteen states. Edmund Pendleton of Virginia explains to a younger countryman that the leaders of the Revolution wanted only a "redress of grievances, not a revolution of government." [18] In other words, they wished matters *put back as they had been*. And James Iredell of North Carolina writes to his angry Loyalist uncle in Jamaica that Americans in 1776 acted only as Englishmen, under an English constitution, even in achieving independence. [19] He continues, "The same principles which led to the steps taken against royal authority [in 1688] would justify any others." [20] Elsewhere Iredell adds that no oath of allegiance to a prince is binding if it is "not consistent with the safety and liberties of the people." Political apologetics in this vein are the commonplace matter of thousands of letters to friends and relatives in England written by new Americans who were still proud of being English and protective of their political inheritance under Burke's version of a constitution. Their originally English voices were also heard in redefining the relation of American beginnings to the great political traditions of the mother country.

The next stage in this process of perpetuation and reembodiment belongs to the period when, while fighting out the Revolution with their kinsmen from Great Britain, our forebears wrote new constitutions for the thirteen former colonies. The notable characteristic of these new constitutions is how little they differed from the charters they emulated and replaced. Willi Paul Adams, the authority on these documents, writes:

> The central role played by British constitutionalism in justifying colonial resistance was carried over into American thinking when the colonies began writing their own in 1776. The basic premise of the colonists' argument was the political order created in 1688, though formulated only in statutes [which appealed to other statutes, petitions, rulings, and charters], could not be changed, even by a majority decision in Parliament approved by the Crown. This English Constitution, the colonists argued, was a permanent code to which the stewards of government power—the King and Parliament—were subject and that they had no authority to alter. [21]

Of course, there were bills of rights in some of these constitutions, and some of them spoke (as the British constitution did not) of human rights—

or at least of rights available to all once they enter into a social condition. Furthermore, a few American radicals had lost their respect for the British constitution before the colonies won their freedom, while others among their countrymen doubted that it was relevant to their problems as citizens of a new republic. The latter opinion was supported even by several members of the Great Convention. Finally, eighteenth-century Americans read the British constitution in several different ways: in the fashion of Blackstone, according to the method of Lord Bolingbroke, or following the manner of David Hume.[22] For some of our forebears, the British constitution was an illustration of the medieval doctrine of the mixed regime, with the great estates of King, Lords, and Commons interacting with and through each other. Others interpreted the same evidence so as to find in the British tradition an even greater protection against tyranny in the separation of executive, legislative, and judicial power. Yet another, smaller group was convinced that the secret of their inheritance from the mother country was to be found in the balance between "country" and "court" parties. Despite this variety of interpretive strategies employed by the Framers, they understood the ancestral constitution and used it in different ways, according to their political assumptions.

There is a temptation to prescind from this spread of evidence an attenuation of British constitutionalism among George III's erstwhile subjects in North America. Yet even in the first years of their collective existence as part of a new political order (*novus ordo seclorum*), most thoughtful Americans invoked the British constitution primarily to explain why the Articles of Confederation would not be enough to foster their country's tenuous internal order, inner strength, and social cohesion. They, however, expected even after revisions in Philadelphia that their government, once reformed, would probably continue to preserve the pattern of jealously independent colonies in tension with a distant and high-handed central authority. Though the federal government would not be so far away as Whitehall or, with its power to tax directly, so restricted in its influence, it was perpetually on trial, thanks to the nature of federalism itself and by virtue of its status as the creation of the sovereign people of the sovereign states. Americans in 1783–86 enjoyed spinning out arguments about the justice of their resistance to tyranny and thus about the proper role of British law in their lives while they had been British subjects. Particularly in New England, the great men of law (Theophilus Parsons, Francis Dana, James Bowdoin, Theodore Sedgwick) feared that the Revolution would continue beyond independence into "democratic excesses." John Adams, especially, admired the fundamental law of Great Britain, describing it as "the most stupendous fabric of human invention" and a greater source of "honor to human understanding" than any other artifact in the "history of civilization."[23] In this discourse, over against Captain Shays and his "rebellion," stands the authority of the stable social teaching of the British constitution. Adams's opinion of the value of a mixed constitution summarizes his region's commitment to English continuity, especially as he writes of these subjects in *A Defence of the Constitutions of Government of the United States of America.*[24]

References to the British constitution are scattered throughout the records of the Great Convention and in the pamphlet literature surrounding that assembly. Indeed, they occurred so frequently that some of the delegates—who in many respects preferred to emulate the British example—registered complaints about their number. These references are basically of two kinds: those that assume the complete usefulness of comparisons to English originals, even when they are incomplete and partially misleading; and those that object to too much dependence on antique analogies and blind retrospection, even though they recognize their role in the convention. For John Dickinson, the British constitution was a "singular and admirable mechanism," a creation of the national experience, which is always of more value than the fruits of a priori rational speculation.[25] Charles Pinckney called it "the best Constitution in Existence."[26] Edmund Randolph spoke of its "excellent fabric," which he hoped the Framers would copy to the best of their ability.[27] The point is that such sentiments are a major component of the discourse within the Great Convention, not exceptional Anglophile outbursts. Forrest McDonald writes, "Whatever their political philosophies, most (though by no means all) of the delegates sought to pattern the United States Constitution, as closely as circumstances would permit, after the English constitution."[28] What is most clear about affirmative comments on America's continuing link to a British inheritance is that they focus on the advantages of the mixed regime, with roots reaching all the way back into medieval history, and that they predicate within that inheritance a level of political liberty and shared self-respect not easily preserved in a simple political structure—monarchy, democracy, or oligarchy—of any of the classical varieties. Invariably, whether the speakers were Federalist or Antifederalist, the leitmotif in their song of praise for inherited ways, modes, and institutions was preserving a balance of liberty with order that can be sustained against enemies within and without: a balance provided in the eighteenth-century British constitution through a sovereign law, coming down from the Magna Carta, the Forest Charters, the Petition of Right, and the Bill of Rights, and a distribution of power between King, Lords, and Commons, mixing the characteristics of various kinds of government.[29]

In both the Great Convention and *The Federalist*, there are extensive comparisons of the American president as chief executive with the functions of the British Crown, and of the House of Representatives with the House of Commons.[30] In these debates and apologetics, differences are developed to show our system as a perfection of its prototype, not as a rejection of the patrimony. In a passage of even more startling applicability to this exposition, John Dickinson of Delaware draws a direct comparison between the United States Senate and the House of Lords—since senators are expected to have a long tenure in office, to represent "rank," property, and establishment, and to check the democratic enthusiasms of a directly elected lower house. According to Dickinson, senators would represent territory, *places*, as do the peers of England, but not populations, becoming "as near as may be to the House of Lords in England."[31] When the architects of our political identity as a people both one and many set out to define their enterprise, they turned to the constitution of Great Britain as it stood from 1688 to 1750 and to their own colonial experience under that constitution—not to Greek leagues, Holland, Venice, Switzerland, and Genoa; not even (though they respected it immensely) to the Roman constitution under the Republic. Naturally they looked first closer to home and merged the lessons from other quarters into their readings of Anglo-American history. But what they might think and how far they might reach toward a republic of abstract proposition and ideological purpose was greatly limited thereby.

What sounds in all this Old Whig music is, of course, not the individualistic sirens' song of Locke or the French philosophes but the organ tones of Bracton, Fortescue, Sir Matthew Hale, Sir Edward Coke, and the independent gentlemen who preserved the Magna Carta, framed the Petition of Right, and required *An Answer to Nineteen Propositions* from Charles I: the tradition of the mixed regime, the balanced constitution, in which *Lex* is *Rex*—the law (meaning the nation's soul, embodied in customs and charters, expectations and language) as sovereign, rooted in the very nature of things. That kind of law is a continuum, an unfolding harmony that, as Ellis Sandoz argues, identifies the American Revolution and its lawgiving aftermath as the last event in Renaissance political history. The beginnings of its modern antitype, of another, more abstract species of law, came a few years later in France with the Rights of Man and Citizen Robespierre.[32] When Gouverneur Morris, Charles Pinckney, Dickinson, Hamilton, Randolph, Pierce Butler, George Mason, and James Madison invoked the British constitution among their fellow Framers, they were merely recalling their more speculative colleagues to a known and recognized norm that no amount of theoretical ingenuity could have contrived, and to a limited, anti-abstractionist view of their lawmaking function. So much of the question before them had been settled long before they were born. That such was a view most of them accepted can be proved from the Constitution they assembled—even though they were very proud of how much they had incidentally improved on the original (in such achievements as a solution to the problem of extended republics) and of the way in which they had converted it into a mutually binding text, with a negative on both the states and the central power.

After the United States Constitution had been drafted and sent out for examination by the states, British constitutional history became a major influence on how it was interpreted by both advocates and adversaries. In North Carolina, Massachusetts, and New York (and in assorted pamphlet literature), pointed comparisons between analogous components of each system were commonplace elements of ratification debates. In Virginia, under the watchcare of Patrick Henry, the inherited rights of English qua American citizens, the chartered rights, became the issue in a criticism of what the Framers had proposed. Moreover, we can see in the fragments of debate preserved from South Carolina that these rights had an equivalent importance there.

Patrick Henry, the most important of the Antifederalists, the man who had set the inertia toward revolution in motion in Virginia as defender of "the spirit of liberty" that Americans "drew . . . from our British ancestors," called the British constitution "the fairest fabric that ever human nature reared." Of the Philadelphia instrument he complains, "there is not an English feature in it." [33] Henry frames his objections to the proposed constitution by declaring: "We are descended from a people whose government was founded on liberty: our glorious forefathers of Great Britain made liberty the foundation of everything. That country is become a great, mighty and splendid nation; not because their government is strong and energetic, but, sir, because liberty is its direct end and foundation." [34] In the same ratifying convention, in support of the handiwork of the Framers, George Nicholas reasoned the other way around: that our Constitution preserves what is of value in the English and also adds improvements. Future president James Monroe, following after Henry's argument, contended, "The wisdom of the English constitution has given a share of legislation to each of the three branches, which enables it effectively to defend itself, and which preserves the liberty of the people of that country." [35] Other Virginians contributed to this same set of invocations, honoring the old authority so as to shape the new.

The variety of Henry's allusions to the British example is extraordinary—almost as if the Revolution had not occurred. But Henry is in no way more surprising than Patrick Dollard of South Carolina during that state's ratification convention, or Francis Kinlock, a fellow Carolinian, in a letter written soon after its conclusion. Dollard, living under the Articles of Confederation in a sovereign South Carolina, still speaks of a "birthright" under the Magna Carta and of how it has been "made over" by friends of the new Constitution.[36] And Kinlock, writing to former Lieutenant Governor Bull two days after he had cast his own vote for ratification, summarizes his view of the implications of the new "bond of Union" with "we are getting back fast to the system we destroyed some years ago." [37] These lines represent only a few of many such passages that survive to us in the ratification records of the various states or in the private correspondence of the Framers.

If there is one constant in the political discourse of eighteenth-century Americans, it is a generous and undeviating admiration for the British constitution as they knew it. Even the greatest theorist whom they recognized, the Baron de Montesquieu, spoke constantly of the merits of the nontheoretical English system. In everything they attempted from 1765 and the quarrel over the Stamp Act through the drafting and adoption of the original United States Constitution in 1787–90 and the addition to it of the Bill of Rights in 1789–91, our forebears invoked the authority of that antecedent constitution as it stood in 1689, following the Glorious Revolution. Neither war nor independence diminished this relationship. In the opinion of many scholars, it is an explanation of the essential character of our fundamental law as a sovereign power, expressive of the deliberate sense of the American people, binding them in a lasting way to an inheritance of specific rights and limited governmental authority that runs all the way back to the Great Charter affirmed in 1215 at Runnymede.

It is impossible to understand what the Framers attempted with the Constitution of the United States without first recognizing why most of them dreaded pure democracy, judicial tyranny, or absolute legislative supremacy and sought instead to secure for themselves and their posterity the sort of specific, negative, and procedural guarantees that have grown up within the context of that (until recently) most stable and continuous version of the rule of law known to the civilized world: the premise that every free citizen should be protected by the law of the land. Sir William Holdsworth, in his *History of English Law*, contrasts the spirit that we discover in the apologies for the American Revolution and the ideological flavor of what its authors said about making the original United States Constitution. He writes in summary that the latter company "went for inspiration to the eighteenth-century British Constitution, with which they were familiar." In another context he expands this idea:

> [The United States Constitution was] built up by skilful adaptation
> to a new situation, of sound institutional traditions derived to some
> extent from the old relations formerly existing between Great Brit-

ain and her American colonies and to a large extent from the British Constitution. . . .

They [the Framers] were not inclined to entrust unfettered powers to a popularly elected legislature; for they recognized that the usurpations of such a legislature would lead to tyranny as quickly as usurpations of the Executive. They were not believers in equalitarian theories.[38]

On the basis of the evidence I have found, Sir William cannot be disputed; and his is the general opinion of other British authorities on the subject.[39] For early English constitutional history is a universe of discourse, a structure of values inherent in the language of its expression that is the opposite of metaphysical speech concerning abstract moral principles and ideal regimes. In other words, it is well suited to the articulation and protection of what the English political theorist Michael Oakeshott speaks of as "nomocratic" orders—those better defined by an established way of conducting their business than by a set of goals.[40] The opposite is found in "teleocratic" regimes, which attempt to embody some large idea such as Justice, Liberty, or Equality in an always incomplete, ever more insistent, process. About this kind of government we know more than we would like. Thinking about the difference between the familiar intellectual context of contemporary ideological politics and what the Framers intended in the way of limited government, we may, even at the distance of two hundred years, recognize how far we have come from those origins, away from securing "the blessings of liberty to ourselves and our posterity." How far, and at what cost.

3

The Process of Ratification:
A Study in Political Dynamics

Even as we, in our own time, go about revising, or refusing to revise, our fundamental law, so did our forebears in the beginning vote to put such law in its place: that is, one state at a time, reflecting, after vigorous dispute, thirteen different majorities, some of them very belated—and very reluctant. All of which is to say that there is no better definition of American Federalism than the process with which that Federalism began: no purely ideological explanation. Yet, though it is true that most American citizens living in 1787 wished to see a revision of the Articles of Confederation, it is a great mistake to assume that a general approval of the Philadelphia Convention and what it had produced was automatic from September 17 of that year onward. Those who know politics cannot believe that a second convention or a circulation of previous amendments was unthinkable, or that outright defeat could not have been arranged. Though some change in the form of government administered by the Continental Congress was, sooner or later, bound to occur, it might have been much less ambitious than what the Framers proposed; and much narrower in the range of implications than even the most subtle constitutional lawyer could wring out of its text. Most obviously, such would have been the case had the state ratifying conventions met in an order somewhat different from the one that history records.

There are, of course, many ways of explaining the sequence of events that provides us with the original Constitution of the United States and then adds to it the supplement that we call (after its British prototype) the "Bill of Rights." Even though they appear to be mutually exclusive, it may be argued of these views that several of them contain a modicum of truth— so far as they go. From two or three I will borrow details in developing the argument that I propose. But through my own study of the records of the Great Convention and of the state ratifications that followed the deliberations in Philadelphia, I have come to believe that it is dangerous and misleading to dump all of these documents together in some great political "stew." Each convention is a dramatic event with a pattern of its own and a meaning determined not only by the special history of the people it represented but also by its function in a larger temporal sequence that cannot be recognized unless the integrity of its components is acknowledged before description begins.

As I believe I have demonstrated in print, no one is more convinced of the uniqueness of particular conventions, of their authority as readings of the fundamental law; no one is more interested in the formal, dramatic view of the Philadelphia Convention itself than I am.[1] It is an action, a form commenting in structure on the bond of union that it produced. Even so, I take separate readings as only a preliminary part of the task of commentary on the making of our Constitution—and attempt to keep in mind that there was, beneath a tiresome pattern of topical squabbling and theoretical dispute, a deeper level of practical consensus so widespread as to require almost no mention in any assembly that occurred during the months when ratification was in question: a consensus that made our forebears, by negation, one people, united in their suspicion of government, of its self-importance, its affected benevolence, its disposition to tyranny established and imposed in the name of "good causes."

A narrative explanation of the political dynamic that finally approved the original Constitution must begin, of course, with the condition of the country after the achievement of independence. A first predicate of this story is the common pride born out of the "sharing" of warfare and of "lesser" perils that produced among men of every opinion a repository of natural fellow-feeling. The seemingly miraculous confirmation of what

Americans had said about themselves, together, through the Continental Congress, in the Declaration of Independence, made possible in 1783 their acceptance of a formal connection in the Articles of Confederation. A common enemy and comradeship in arms are not a poor basis for political cooperation. The Confederation, however, proved to be only a temporary expedient, a stop-gap measure for use in effecting a transition to some more durable, self-sufficient bond.

By 1786 independence had brought economic problems, both within the country and in the difficulty of its citizens in doing business overseas. Furthermore, there were Indian insurgencies along a now open frontier, problems with foreign debt, problems with opportunistic internal tariffs interrupting interstate commerce, a large domestic debt, and a pattern of domestic insurrections coming to a head with Captain Daniel Shays's "Rebellion" in Massachusetts during the fall and winter of 1786–87. Though not a veritable "sea of troubles," most Americans blamed most of these conditions on the incapacities of the government put in place by the Articles of Confederation and were, before the Philadelphia Convention gathered in May 1787, ready for a new compact that served at least those purposes described as the proper objectives of the Framers by Roger Sherman of Connecticut: (1) defense against foreign danger; (2) control of internal disputes and disorders; (3) treaties; (4) foreign commerce; and (5) a revenue to be derived from it.[2] Mild Federalists such as Pierce Butler, William Samuel Johnson, John Rutledge, Edmund Pendleton, William R. Davie, Oliver Ellsworth, Hugh Williamson, Richard Dobbs Spaight, and Abraham Baldwin embodied the same conflicting but balanced impulses toward cohesion and dispersal that we find in the thought of Sherman, and in the attitudes of such mild Antifederalists as James Monroe, William Paca, Melancton Smith, Elbridge Gerry, and Eliphalet Dyer. It therefore was certain that something would be done, but not too much—that no remote, arbitrary, and sometimes unfriendly sovereign would be created to replace the remote, arbitrary, and sometimes unfriendly power whose authority they had just escaped.

There were, to be sure, versions of Federalism much more ambitious than what we see in Roger Sherman's little list, dreams of union theoretically and ideologically instrumental in their intention to form a purposive state, something grand and imperial. These plans belonged to Alexander Hamilton, James Wilson, Gouverneur Morris, Robert Morris—and James Madison. By reminding their countrymen of a politics they had just escaped, they threatened ratification. And there were a few Antifederalists who wished to continue under the Articles as they stood, or with very minor modification to guarantee a revenue: the men of Rhode Island, John Francis Mercer of Maryland, General Samuel Thompson of Massachusetts, President Rawlins Lowndes of South Carolina, Mayor John Lansing of Albany, New York, and (perhaps) Patrick Henry himself. Such men were straightforward impediments to "a more perfect Union." But the most serious obstacles in the path of the Constitution were of another kind, coming from other quarters, and were more circumstantial and strategic than substantive in their character. We have all heard that, in politics, timing is of the essence—*when* and not *which measures*. The ratification of the United States Constitution within the context I have just described is an illustration of that principle.

By and large, the first states that voted in favor of the Constitution made in Independence Hall created very little momentum tending in its direction. No current flowed from these decisions. Nothing doctrinal or intellectually substantial was decided by such approvals as were given by Delaware (December 7, 1787), New Jersey (December 18, 1787), Georgia (January 2, 1788), and Connecticut (January 9, 1788); or even by a later affirmation in Maryland (April 28, 1788). Because of immediate dangers— economic, social, or military—faced by these communities, they were inclined to go along with any plan of government that would protect their commerce from the drain of interstate duties and/or the depredations of savage raiders. Connecticut wanted to avoid disorders such as were spreading just beyond its borders—in Rhode Island, Massachusetts, and New Hampshire. It also wanted security for lands promised to it in the Western Reserve of Ohio and relief from the cost of doing business through the port of New York. Pennsylvania had (December 12, 1787), thanks to its great men of business and banking, an image of all the fine things a stronger government might do or encourage. Philadelphia defined Pennsylvania Federalism—and kept the western counties of the state in check. Everyone expected ratification from these sources.

Voting for the Constitution in commonwealths that might have done otherwise was another matter. Such decisions in Massachusetts and South Carolina, states jealous of their own established identities, with each of them deeply suspicious of what the other represented, had a direct impact on the potential recalcitrance of other Northern and Southern communities. On terms that they dictated in reading the Constitution in a certain way, these ratifications made for the instruction of stubborn Antifederalists who persisted in seeing a Leviathan hidden just underneath the innocuous surface of its text. They were a step toward the accomplishment of the ends of a national connection as these states conceived of them: a version that left forever secure the corporate liberty of Zion and the erstwhile Palmetto Republic, left them free to continue in character—even though they were to do so within a political combination, by way of that combination. Down in Charleston, the heroic Rawlins Lowndes drew all of this matter, a full teaching on the Constitution, from his numerous Federalist adversaries. They defined the instrument of government that they were advocating over against a version less sanguine and less tolerable—the basis of Lowndes's extraordinary prophecies. In Massachusetts the Jeremiahs were more numerous. And also their respondents. But the warnings of tyranny that Antifederalists offered and the affirmations used to answer them followed the same pattern that we can trace out from the Carolina legislative debates of January 1788 in which, these two hundred years ago, the lowcountry came together to risk a commitment to union.[3]

In New York, Virginia, and North Carolina, the power of Federalist example in other conventions is reflected directly in local ratification debates. John Kaminski, editor of *The Documentary History of the Ratification of the Constitution*, has written of the July 1788 Federalist victory in the Empire State that, despite a more than 2 to 1 Antifederalist advantage in delegate commitments, "It was felt that all of the ratifying states could not be wrong, and therefore the Constitution should be given a chance."[4] In the second volume of Elliot's *Debates*, we read of the impact in the convention at Poughkeepsie of word that a ninth state has ratified, and the assumption that such information would change the pattern of events in New York. There are related statements in the records of the Virginia convention concluded in Richmond on June 25, 1788, and an even more telling remark in the North Carolina convention of later that summer. There Governor Samuel Johnston responds to exaggerated Antifederalist fears for what the Constitution will do to the public liberty now that "states who have been as jealous of their liberties as any in the world have adopted it."[5] Massachusetts and South Carolina acted because their leaders had been convinced during the Revolution that they needed to be part of a larger American entity in order to preserve the cherished integrity of their own ways of life. What they decided influenced similar decisions made in New Hampshire and North Carolina. But more important, they had influence in Virginia and New York—also states that might have voted "no." That Massachusetts approved meant that New Hampshire finally (June 21, 1788) ratified. And when these were combined with the influence of Virginia, New York also ratified on July 26, 1788. Such events in their turn brought pressure on North Carolina (November 21, 1789) and then, finally, on Rhode Island (May 29, 1790). Sequence, not the power of persuasion or the force of political arguments, is the key to this narrative, the kind of "bandwagon" psychology about which any practiced politician knows a good deal. But the dynamic of these conventions might have been very much otherwise, and with consequences we can hardly imagine. Let us think for a moment about such a hypothetical process, to learn from it a truth about the origins of American politics.

Suppose the struggle over ratification had been governed by a different strategy among the Antifederalists, and New Hampshire and North Carolina had been brought to make early decisions on the Constitution—decisions in the negative. Suppose then further that New York and Virginia had been rushed to judgment immediately following the votes against ratification in the two other states. It is reasonable to assume that one or both of the big Antifederalist strongholds would under such circumstances have also refused to approve the instrument under consideration. Under these circumstances Massachusetts would have voted "no" had it come next in the sequence. Maryland would have followed after Virginia; and nothing would then have served to get Rhode Island to change its mind. In this hypothetical scenario of how ratification could have been prevented, it would signify nothing at all if Delaware, New Jersey, Georgia, and even Pennsylvania continued to approve the Constitution as we know it. Political dynamics are not the same thing as intellectual substance. The best constitution ever devised would be disapproved within a formula for deliberation such as the one designed to test the United States Constitution if the opponents of the plan managed to react to it officially before its supporters were ready to speak up. Democratic politics do not always turn upon judgments of substantive questions so much as they do upon procedural strategies, fashions, and trends. What I say of such politics was almost as true in 1787–88 as it is today. The difference is in *how democratic* the politics are.

Federalists and Antifederalists were not in 1787 organized political parties in the current sense but twenty-six different state parties, thirteen on each side of the general question but not agreed with their allies on much else. In a broad sense, town men and commercial men tended to be Federalists throughout the country. But that distinction does not tell us about what they thought of the proper relation of religion to government, about slavery, John Jay's proposed *entente* with Spain, navigation acts, sumptuary laws, or the origins of liberty in a presocial state. Some Antifederalists wanted a Bill of Rights to protect the individual against untoward intrusions in his private affairs. Most of them, like Patrick Henry and Rawlins Lowndes, wanted only securities for corporate liberty: for the independence of the community to negotiate within itself those values it would affirm. Almost all hoped for the best, once the Constitution had been approved, speaking of it as Charles Pinckney did on May 14, 1788, when he called it "the temple of our freedom—a temple founded in the affections, and supported by the virtue, of the people."[6]

During the various ratifying conventions and in the recommended amendments that brought about the Bill of Rights, the Antifederalists had required their neighbors to specify that there was nothing hidden in the silences of the Constitution, that "everything not granted is reserved." Said Colonel Joseph Varnum of Massachusetts, "no right to alter the internal relations of the states" exists under the new government.[7] To the same effect, his old counterpart Samuel Adams (quoting Governor Hancock) added, "all powers not expressly delegated to Congress are reserved to the several states, to be by them exercised."[8] We hear the same thing from James Wilson of Pennsylvania in his State House Yard Speech of

October 6, 1787; from General William R. Davie of North Carolina; from Justice Iredell of the same state; and from Madison and Pendleton of Virginia and John Lansing of New York—which is only a partial listing of participants in this litany.

That the powers of the new government are few and explicit is in the ratifying conventions the central theme of the Federalist defense of the United States Constitution and a primary explanation of why the sequence of ratifications went as it did. If we would understand these results and the enthusiasm with which an essentially conservative people looked forward with hope to life under the new government that they made possible, then we should find ground for them in "minimalist" interpretations of the authority that was thus created. They are a measure of how different from what was intended our fundamental law has become, and of the difficulty we fall into in attempting to read into it the ideological fashions of our own time. A good sense of the politics of ratification is more to our purpose in construing the meaning of what transpired as we began the adventure story that is our nation's history.

4

A Dike to Fence Out the Flood: The Ratification of the Constitution in Massachusetts

When in September 1787 the new instrument of government proposed by the Great Convention went out from Philadelphia to be received and considered by the several commonwealths connected through the old Articles of Confederation, those fraternally affiliated societies saw the document delivered to them through the Continental Congress according to their own needs and purposes—out of their distinctive histories and established political dispositions. In other words, working from their respective myths of themselves as Americans of a special kind, as Federalists or Antifederalists, the speakers of these societies saw in the prospect of a more perfect Union implications very dissimilar from those discovered by like-minded individuals—persons agreed with them in supporting or opposing the Constitution in other states. Amid the variety of these responses, that of Massachusetts, in both its Federalism and Antifederalism, is distinctive in several respects. Moreover, what was observed concerning the Constitution in the state ratification convention that began in Boston on January 9, 1788, was as detailed, as representative of the essentially local politics that produced it and as thought-provoking as any record of deliberations at this level generated by the great process of lawgiving—of Constitution-making—that has survived to us from those momentous times: a copious and inclusive proceeding, the outcome of which was in doubt almost to the moment of its decision in favor of a revision of the national bond. It is possible to take the text of the Massachusetts ratification and read it as a completed action, a formal structure with complication, peripeteia, and dramatic resolution—in other words, as a literary whole. And by text I mean here the 1856 edition of *Debates and Proceedings in the Convention of the Commonwealth of Massachusetts, Held in the Year 1788, and Which Finally Ratified the Constitution of the United States*, which was printed in Boston according to the will of the state legislature and by William White, printer to the Commonwealth.[1] I have, thanks to friends in New England, the pleasure of owning a copy of this unusual and uniquely valuable book. From a distant and southern perspective, I have found the versions of the ratification story contained in it to be of special interest to the close student of the regional origins of American politics: a window on the sources of our persistent and ultimately admirable national variety. But to understand the action preserved in its pages, the distinctive New England coloring of the event recorded there, it is a necessary predicate for other exegeses that we first reconstruct the milieu in which it occurred and reassemble the context of circumstance within which it was played out and the universe of discourse in the language of which it is preserved for our examination.

Available for application to that end is a substantial body of commentary accounting for the details and the dynamic of the Massachusetts convention itself and of the history antecedent to its gathering in the close quarters of Moorehead's Meeting House on Milk Street—especially the growing discontent that spread across Massachusetts during the summer and fall of 1786 and then exploded in December of that year in the insurrection that we now call (after its eventual leader, Captain Daniel Shays of Pelham) Shays's Rebellion. This list begins with Samuel Bannister Harding's 1896 monograph, *The Contest over the Ratification of the Federal Constitution in the State of Massachusetts.*[2] Excellent supplements to Harding's narrative appear in Van Beck Hall's *Politics Without Parties: Massachusetts, 1780–1791*, and in Robert Allen Rutland's *The Ordeal of the Constitution: The Antifederalists and the Ratification Struggle of 1787–1788.*[3] These accounts are reinforced by Stephen E. Patterson's "The Roots of Massachusetts Federalism: Conservative Political Culture Before 1787" and James M. Banner, Jr.'s *To the Hartford Convention: The Federalists and the Origins of Party Politics in Massachusetts, 1789–1815*; and by a variety of studies that focus as much on Shays's Rebellion as they do on its constitutional aftermath.[4]

What we discover, first of all, from a familiarity with this scholarship, with the transcripts of the Massachusetts convention debates and the political conversations on the same subjects that went on in the twelve other states called upon by the formula of the Framers to make their discrete decisions for dispersion or connection is that the community of the Saints had its own ideas concerning what the new Constitution would mean to the children of the Covenant, what might be said against it or in its behalf. And this version, I shall explain, is in important ways unlike the Constitution spoken of in the states to the south and west of New England—even though the words approved are the same. Part of the reason for this uniqueness is, to be sure, that Shays's Rebellion went on in Massachusetts, ending only in February 1787 at Petersham and Sheffield. Another essentially local influence on the politics of ratification was Massachusetts's exceptional approach to the retirement of state debt—and to the failure of its citizens to pay their taxes levied for that purpose: a moral and political attitude, rooted in its Calvinist origins. But in the end even the disturbance of the courts and taxpayers' revolt acquires much of its resonance because it occurred in the Citadel of the Elect, the Protestant Zion—among a people called out to the special and collective service of God and to the building of His Kingdom in the West, that righteous New Jerusalem which the prophets had foretold. To be in debt was to be under God's judgment, with no sign of special favor—to be divested of a sacred patrimony; it was a situation the Saints could not endure.

Out of the original variety of these ratifications in Massachusetts and less self-conscious communities have come the raw material and inceptional impulse for much of the continuing argument about the intentions embodied in our Constitution, and the obligations they impose upon us even now. The United States Constitution as ratified in Boston on February 6, 1788, continues to have a life among us even greater than the once more popular views of that document approved by the states outside of New England.

T*he best way to reconstruct* and recover the Massachusetts view of the purpose and value of the Constitution is by following seriatim its operations—its unfolding—in that state's ratifying convention: by such sequential analysis, and by a close attention to the special Massachusetts objections to what the fifty-five members of the Great Convention produced. Leaving aside for the moment the direct influence of Puritan origins, the story begins almost a year before the Framers gathered in Philadelphia and exhibits as its central core, its principle of action, the influence of a characteristic New England virtue carried so far into the extreme that it became a vice—a pattern that I understand has had some influence over the history of the region. The virtue of which I speak is frugality. After independence had been achieved and the inhabitants of the old Bay Colony had become accustomed to life under their 1780 Constitution, they began (as was appropriate for the children of the Puritan forebears) to regard the massive proportions of their state debt with embarrassment or even guilt and to look about for ways of lifting this badge of perfidy from their collective backs.[5] Other commonwealths suspended payment on foreign obligations or prepared to satisfy creditors with land or a relaxed and protracted schedule of repayments. But not Massachusetts. The General Court laid on a heavy tax (as opposed to impost or excise charged against trade) that fell in particular on the rural and western portions of the state, on farmers and other holders of real property. All of this occurred in the midst of an agricultural depression. In consequence, the courts of common pleas were filled with suits against landholders whose property would be sold because they made so little profit from it. Compounding these delinquencies was a shortage of specie in circulation, which drove down the price of the farmers' produce and the value of their acres. And that is to say nothing of the expense of litigation if brought to the bar of justice, or of the danger of being imprisoned for debt. The upshot of all of this distress was a cry of outrage that poured in toward Boston from every corner of the state, except for a few commercial communities, fishing towns, or seaports—a cry that began in the summer of 1786 with the calling of local protest conventions gathered to petition the General Court for relief and which had as its final response the outbreak of open revolution against the legal authority of the state of Massachusetts.

The traditional view of Shays's Rebellion in relation to the approval of the Constitution in Massachusetts is that it amounted to the proximate cause of that decision. In the last fifty years alternative explanations of these events and their connection have been advanced; but once refined with observations on the link between social unrest and both Antifederalism and Federalism, the traditional explanation now seems thoroughly vindicated. New Englanders belonged to a culture turned inward on itself, from the failure of the "Good Old Cause" to the beginnings of the "errand into the wilderness." The Revolution broke some of this down. They were forced to send to Virginia for help when General Gage occupied their metropolis. Shays's Rebellion finished their turning toward the business of the new republic, where as inheritors of something valuable they might once again have a role to play and an example to set. It took fifty years for Massachusetts Federalists to get over their fear of marching feet—if indeed they ever have. Yet there had been anxieties and complaints about democratic excesses in the backcountry and the Berkshires even before the infant republics had, together, declared their independence in 1776. And a reaction to these excesses gathered into something like a political party before the end of the Revolutionary War in 1783. A leader of this party, James Bowdoin, was governor of Massachusetts when Shays's Rebellion broke out. He and his friends were responsible for restoring government in those Massachusetts communities where anarchy had usurped its place.

By 1786 Federalist sentiment was openly antidemocratic in its Massachusetts variety. The redoubtable Theodore Sedgwick, later to become United States senator and Speaker of the United States House of Representatives, wrote to Rufus King, as they contemplated the spectacle of popular uprising against the people's government: "Every man of observation is convinced that the end of government security cannot be attained by the exercise of principles founded on democratic equality. A war is now levied on the virtue, property and distinctions in the community, and however there may be an appearance of a temporary cessation of hostilities, yet the flame will again and again break out." [6] Fisher Ames, while on the floor of the Massachusetts ratification convention itself, spoke to the same effect as his friend Sedgwick (but more colorfully) when he declared, "A democracy is a volcano, which conceals the fiery materials of its own destruction. These will produce an eruption, and carry desolation in their way." [7]

Ames was quietly but ably supported by the Reverend Thomas Thacher, who warned the spokesmen for popular resentment to remember the connection between "licentiousness" and tyranny; who spoke of disturbances similar to Shays's Rebellion in other American states; and who insisted that "demagogues, in all free governments, have at first held out an idea of extreme liberty and have seized on the rights of the people under the mask of patriotism." [8] Federalists rang the changes on one important theme: that "faction and enthusiasm are the instruments by which popular governments are destroyed." Unreasonable expectations had brought on "an anarchy, and that leads to tyranny." On the other hand, common enemies and a concern for the "common interest" foster liberty. [9] The Constitution was a way of preserving a known felicity, not a means of achieving a new one. If everyone at the convention recognized that the objections of the Antifederalists to the document would probably be raised against any replacement for it that would be approved by a convention of the states, how could they continue to resist the imperative to ratify: "Do they expect one which will not annul the Confederation, or that the persons and properties of the people shall not be included in the compact, and that we shall hear no more about armies and taxes?" [10] Antifederalists might complain that Ames and his friends were fostering a "backlash" reaction to popular unrest, that they encouraged the people to "run mad with loyalty." [11] But the Massachusetts tradition of ordered liberty was ever stronger than anger with lawyers and speculators in public debt. The dead voted yes on the Constitution—and were powerful enough to carry the day.

Shaysites, who were usually less radical than their opponents made them out to be, and who wanted chiefly, for all their troublesome noise, no more than tax relief, lower legal fees, and a better circulation of money, appear in Federalist literature as serious "levellers" and outright egalitarians. There is a little evidence to support such a reading of Rhode Island Antifederalism, of the mob that interrupted a session of the New Hampshire legislature in September 1786, and of the extreme radicals who wished to move the state capital from Boston and marched to Springfield to prevent the opening of the state courts in January 1787: a law which proposed that "at the end of thirteen years . . . there be a general abolition of debts, and an equal distribution of property"; talk at Exeter of holding "all things in common"; a report of the opinion of a Shaysite that, as all the property of the nation had been defended by all the people, it ought therefore "to be the common property of all" — with anyone who objected to this creed "to be swept from the face of the earth." [12] Several members of the Massachusetts ratification convention expressed a concern that the rights of the people might not be properly protected by the new Constitution. [13] Others seemed to fear that the new fundamental law might cancel securities provided for in Massachusetts's own Bill of Rights. Federalists responded with clear distinctions concerning the roles of state and general government. Governor Bowdoin is most explicit: "With regard to rights, the whole Constitution is a declaration of rights, which primarily and principally respect the general government intended to be formed by it. The rights of particular States and private citizens not being the object or subject of the Constitution, they are only incidentally mentioned." [14]

Colonel Joseph Varnum agreed that Congress had "no right to alter the internal regulations of a State." [15] He was supported by the learned Theophilus Parsons, who "demonstrated the impracticability of forming a bill, in a national Constitution, for securing individual rights." [16] And by the durable Sedgwick, who wrote to a friend, "Had the national government undertaken to guaranty the several rights of citizenship contained in their [the states'] declaratory bills, it would have given a right of interference which would naturally tend to check, circumscribe and finally annihilate all state power." [17] Joining in this chorus is, unexpectedly, Samuel Adams, first of the Sons of Liberty and prospective spokesman for the Antifederalist cause — until his son dies, his supporters in Boston turn Federalist, and John Hancock decides to be a hero one time more. Speaking of proposed amendments, he affirms the one which provides "that it be explicitly declared, that all powers not expressly delegated to Congress are reserved to the several States, to be by them exercised." Says Adams, "This appears to my mind to be a summary of the bill of rights." [18] There were, of course, stubborn radicals who remained unsatisfied with the promise of federalism, part of a population filled with an "inordinate self-confidence" in "their ability to pass upon the most abstruse questions of government."[19] The Constitution would have been refused in Virginia, New York, and elsewhere if the Massachusetts Antifederalists had, out of their resentment of Federalist leaders (of wealth, education, lawyers) and the rigorous punitive aftermath of Shays's Rebellion, prevented its approval in their state.[20] Probably they could have been successful if their natural leadership had been elected to serve in the convention.[21] But Gerry and Warren and Winthrop lived in townships where the Constitution was admired and were thus denied a seat. And other Antifederalists kept quiet or did not even bother to stand for election. From the first, what worked most against the Federalist cause (apart from "the apparently vindictive way in which the [Bowdoin] government in Boston had disfranchised and prosecuted the Shaysites after their surrender") had been Massachusetts's fierce insularity; a powerful spirit of localism; the advantage belonging to well-tested "manners," modes, and orders; the general American fear of remote and hostile authorities compounded to the third power by an attendant pride in being part of a "chosen" people—who even lived longer than citizens of other American regions, so wholesome was their place of habitation.[22] And, with that group pride, presuming a common patrimony and blood, went a corporate hostility to contamination working inward from the perimeters of Zion, to a dilution or "thinning out" of the Puritan substance by reason of being "unequally yoked together" with assorted godless heathen. Consolidation, in the opinion of Benjamin Randall, "would introduce manners among us which would set us at continual variance."[23] Worse than "the pirates of Algiers" or "the haughty Spaniard" were the wicked Southerners: "We shall suffer from joining with them." Or, what is worse, "We shall be slaves to the Southern states."[24] General William Heath, in reaction to this evidence of an exclusive spirit, asks his neighbors, "shall we refuse to eat or to drink, or to be united, with those who do not think or act just as we do?" To the proposition that "the interests of the States are too dissimilar for a Union," Federalists say little more than that "the members of the southern States, like ourselves, have *their* prejudices."[25] At times the complaint is aimed at the luxury of life in the

South, where two days' work stands in the place of six in Essex County. In other circumstances there are objections to slavery, both as a violation of essential human liberty and as a flight from the life of industry. General Samuel Thompson thunders, "If the southern States would not give up the right of slavery, then we should not join with them."[26] To this line of thought Caleb Strong replies, "The southern States have their inconveniences; none but negroes can work there."[27] Strong reminds the Massachusetts delegates of the superiority of the New England "way." And if slavery will not do for a danger, how about Popery and the Inquisition?[28] That complaining of one violation of essential human liberties while recommending another kind of repression is, of course, contradictory. It is also in keeping with an essential paradox of Massachusetts history and reduces natural grumbling against three-fifths of the slaves being counted in the political census of states and districts to the level of a mere irritant, brought on by the unwholesome situation of those folk "down there." Yet even with sectionalism under control, Massachusetts Federalists were not ready for a vote; they therefore kept the conversation going, even though by continuing they ran a risk of sharpening the most serious of Antifederalist fears — that they will collect money "by the point of the sword," "heavy direct taxes" of the kind that had spawned Shays's Rebellion in the first place.[29]

Because they had such a numerical advantage when the convention first assembled (as many as forty-eight votes), Antifederalists set the tone of the meeting. The business of that assembly was, to be sure, not so much disinterested deliberation as it was to hear what everyone knew would be a vigorous case put against the Constitution and then to see what kind of circumstantial argument might issue from its friends and champions. The convention worked through the Constitution and stopped for discussion only as objections were voiced. Its delays bought time for the Federalists, who would have been defeated in any division of the House in early January, but did not guarantee their success at a later date. Despite delays, the Antifederalists had a great strategic advantage in that they spoke not for the Articles of Confederation but for the integrity of Massachusetts, the state's sense of itself, "since our fathers dug clams at Plymouth," embodied in much of the dialogue between critics and supporters of the Constitution.[30] The task of the Federalists was to persuade those less-than-certain delegates that the best way to save the Commonwealth they all professed to love was by accepting, on balance, a Constitution all knew to be imperfect. Federalists sometimes made a normative argument for union per se but not forcefully for this particular version of union. It was only "as good a Constitution of government as the people would bear."[31]

Finally it became obvious to James Bowdoin, Rufus King, Nathaniel Gorham, and Theophilus Parsons, who had more or less organized the Federalist forces, that some concession to Antifederalist objections would have to be made — a concession in the form of recommended amendments. And Governor Hancock (elected president of the convention but waiting at home — with the excuse of poor health — to see which way the wind blew) was brought in to support that concession as a sufficient protection for self-government in Massachusetts. It appears that a delegation of Federalists went to see the governor with this rhetorical package, offering him the opportunity to lead them forward toward what inevitably was their future while continuing to honor the history, the identity of his people: a chance to be the central player in a melodrama. The Federalists would provide what Gouverneur Morris spoke of as "loaves and fishes" — a miracle of persuasion to bring around popular politicians — as part of the arrangement; they were (reported Rufus King) obliged to promise Hancock no opposition to his reelection and, in addition, the possibility that he might (if George Washington were unavailable) become President of the United States.[32] Hancock appears to have become a good Federalist in no time at all. His true motives and perceptions in these rapid developments remain a mystery at the heart of the Massachusetts convention. Clearly he knew that the tradesmen and mechanics agreed with the merchants and gentry of the populous areas of the state; and he must have realized that the Articles would be revised or replaced, one way or another. Therefore, taking nine amendments authored by Parsons and King (a distillate of the most valid Antifederalist objections to the Constitution), Hancock, on January 31, came to the floor of the convention and moved the twenty-plus votes needed to ensure ratification: moved them by reserving powers not expressly delegated; by providing one representative to every thirty thousand persons; by restraining the authority of Congress to supervise elections; by outlawing direct taxes unless the impost and excise are insufficient; by forbidding favorable treatment to a particular company of merchants; by withdrawing federal judicial authority over disputes of a certain size between citizens of two different states; by providing for trial by jury in civil cases, when desired; by guaranteeing grand jury indictments as a precondition for a certain order of trials; and by strengthening the prohibition against titles of nobility.[33]

After this surprise, Samuel Adams (with only a moment's deviation) decided to support the Constitution himself. Thereafter the convention concluded swiftly—by a vote of 187 to 168—to the great satisfaction of those Federalist managers who had done such a good job in counting the House. Writing to his old friend Washington, General Benjamin Lincoln, one of his state's most substantial citizens, observed, "Considering the great disorders that took place in the State the last winter, and considering the great influence that the spirit which then reigned has had since, and considering, also, that when we came together a very decided majority of the Convention were against adopting the Constitution, we have got through the business pretty well."[34]

After having followed it all the way back to its colonial sources in Massachusetts politics and then forward from its opening salvos through the drama of resolution by crafty stage managers in a flamboyant *deus ex machina*, it remains for me to say something about the ethos, the special flavor of ratification in Massachusetts, of the human ingredients that brought the Commonwealth out of its jealously guarded particularity by an appeal to its own intellectual inheritance: by persuading descendants of the Puritans that the best way to preserve their little world was by subsuming for it a place in the Union. After ratification, many of the Massachusetts Antifederalists promised before they left for home to urge their neighbors to give the new Constitution a fair trial. Though accustomed to having their say and to being consulted in the public business, the ordinary citizens of Zion represented by so many plain men who had in most cases come there to prevent deception through hasty ratifying were justified in feeling, once the convention was concluded, that a thorough ventilation of the issues had occurred. And with that ventilation, as the Federalists would have insisted, an even more thorough examination of many non-issues that were injected into the debates by the spirit of excessive political distrust—a danger of which the Reverend Thacher had warned pointedly in his memorable address.

Because of Shays's Rebellion and because of the notorious sensitivity of the Massachusetts electorate, the educated and powerful men of the seacoast, the professions and commercial towns were patient in answering their Antifederalist adversaries when these little-known but emphatic speakers conjured up dreadful possibilities and "worst-possible-case" scenarios based upon a strange reading of the most innocuous components of the Constitution. What was the new government going to do with the ten square miles of the federal district? What engines of war and hosts of mercenaries might be assembled there in a plot against the liberties of the people? And if General Benjamin Lincoln and Governor James Bowdoin had been hard on poor fellows who neglected to pay their tax, what would the gathered power, the standing army of a national government, do in the same cause—especially if their taxes were going to redeem at a hundred cents on the dollar government notes that its friends (inside traders) had acquired at a fraction of that price? To the uninitiated, it would seem that the Massachusetts convention spent an inordinate amount of time talking about annual elections, far too much energy in worrying about how Congress might use its power to cancel the ability of Massachusetts to govern itself. And there was some excited talk about slavery and the absence of a religious test for office, issues discussed below. But seen as a whole, the proceedings of this convention, held under these trying circumstances, seem to me quite amiable, with only here and there the edges of acrimony in sight. All of the members of the convention are aware that they have been given a part in a momentous occasion, and they do not waste many of the theatrical opportunities provided for them on this stage of history. It is difficult to imagine a more rhetorically self-conscious assembly. Even the plainest member does his best to argue from authority, *ad vericundium*. Sometimes they even mention with surprise how well they speak. And the danger of being subjected to an apostrophe is apparent from every quarter of the house.[35] We hear of how Thomas Dawes makes only a "short exordium" to his remarks; of how Nathaniel Barrell of York is "sensible" of how "little" he must appear "in the eyes of those giants in rhetoric, who have exhibited such a pompous display of declamation." [36] And of how the Honorable Amos Singletary is suspicious of the arts of "these lawyers, the men of learning, and moneyed men, that talk so finely, and gloss over matters so smoothly, to make us poor, illiterate people swallow down the pill." [37] This sort of complaint against rhetoric is proof positive that the Antifederalists had a lively rhetoric of their own, a populist idiom that they used to considerable effect when not attempting to imitate and better the Federalists at their own game.

But what may surprise us most about this ratifying convention is not the rhetoric of its members but the language itself, the shifting levels of discourse, the apt allusion, the mixture of homely materials with elevated concerns and definitions, and the unmistakable personal dynamic of a society with a well-developed sense of itself. As we would expect, adversions to the Holy Scripture are a staple of these exchanges. But they are set alongside fresh imagery, fragments of irritation, candor, hyperbole, understatement, sarcasm, drollery, and a suggestion of assorted parables working at the back of the minds of most of the delegates who gathered that winter in Boston to decide the fate of the document made in Philadelphia during the previous summer. We have the compass to take note of only a few illustrations of this lively and indigenous speech—an idiom shared by all of those who sat within the closed and comforting circle, inside the walls of John Winthrop's "City on a Hill."

I will begin my list with phrases from General Samuel Thompson, one of the most stubborn of the Antifederalists, who speaks of being ready to give a good "thump" to the provision for regulating elections by Congress: a test of the kind given by country folk to melons to see if they are ripe. [38] Elsewhere the good general warns of the danger of building on a "sandy foundation" and of swallowing "a large bone for the sake of a little meat." [39] His counterpart, the Honorable Amos Singletary, complains that the Federalists "play round the subject with their fine stories, like a fox round a trap." [40] Benjamin Randall of Sharon, in response to the theory that the institution of slavery would end in 1808, said that the southerners "would call us pumpkins" if they heard reports of such speculation. [41] Captain Isaac Snow argued in behalf of ratification that the imbecility of government under the Articles had caused this country to be "held in the same light by foreign nations as a well-behaved negro in a gentleman's family."[42] In other situations, delegates drew upon images of "clouds" rising upon the horizon, of facing the "musket of death."[43] They referred to themselves as "plough-joggers" and compared government to farming—with the proposed Constitution being like a barrier erected to keep the wild beasts out of the new ground.[44] They traveled over the text from the first word to the last and gave it the "thump" General Thompson promised.

Yet assuredly more important than this folk speech is the way in which the members of the Massachusetts convention drew upon the idiom of the English Bible. As did no other state ratification convention, the proceedings in Massachusetts presumed the theological doctrine that God deals collectively with the tribes and nations of men as they exist in the world—according to the operations of His covenant with them, if they have a rightful fear of the Lord. On this assumption, the Honorable Charles Turner of Scituate shortly before the final vote was taken invokes "that God, who has always in a remarkable manner watched over us and our fathers for good, in all difficulties, dangers and distresses."[45] His authority in this instance is what James M. Banner, Jr., calls "the myth of New England exclusiveness"; a set of "ideals at whose core was the conviction that the people of New England, and none more than those of Massachusetts, were somehow set apart from the nation" in their particular intimacy with the Deity.[46] On these grounds the members of the Massachusetts convention sometimes referred to their Commonwealth as if it were another Israel—and the sayings and stories in Holy Writ material drawn from the lives of their neighbors or the neighbors of their forebears. When Barrell compares a rush toward final judgment of the Constitution to the "driving of Jehu, very furiously," he invokes for frame of reference an entire narrative (II Kings 9:20) of two kings of Israel and two of Judah who rule after the fall of that wicked prince Ahab.[47] Elsewhere, General Washington is compared to Joshua and the people of Massachusetts to Jonah swallowed up by the great Leviathan of government.[48] To a contrary effect, the Reverend Isaac Backhus discoursed learnedly of I Corinthians: "Ye are bought with a price."[49]

The new covenant is for free people. Free people might argue yea or nay about the omission of a religious test for holders of federal office.

They might defend either liberty or authority with a view to the common good. And in this "Protestant" fashion they worked their way through the proposed Constitution, comparing ancient and modern times, passage with passage, after the practice of "elucidating scripture with scripture."[50] When Jones of Bristol suggested there was not enough of the old Puritan spirit in their proceedings and proposed that the convention adjourn for a period of fasting and adoration, his colleagues did not agree with him, even though they knew that the politicians of their time were not "better now than when men after God's own heart did wickedly."[51] But when they pulled together their final apology for the revision of government under the United States Constitution, the Federalists of Massachusetts, even more than those of Connecticut and New Hampshire, spoke of an enterprise in the language of covenant theory, postulating a regime that would preserve the Saints, with their liberties, together—or not at all.

The classic text for the corporate theory of Massachusetts Federalism is the one from which I draw the title for these remarks. It is of course the work of the brilliant Fisher Ames, much of it offered just at the close of the Massachusetts convention on February 5, 1788. In content it is as rich in metaphor and as vibrantly colorful as any of the overheated warnings of the opponents of the Constitution: "Who is there that really loves liberty, that will not tremble for its safety, if the Federal government should be dissolved? Can liberty be safe without government? The period of our political dissolution is approaching. Anarchy and uncertainty attend our future state; but this we know, that liberty, which is the soul of our existence, once fled, can return no more."[52] Ames then continues with his tropes. The Union is the "sap that nourishes the trees." Once girdled, it will molder and "be torn down by the tempest." Massachusetts cannot secure its fisheries or its trade by itself, or defend itself alone from external enemies almost as dangerous as the anarchy within. Then the great peroration: "We talk as if there were no danger in deciding wrong. But when the inundation comes, shall we stand on dry land? The State government is a beautiful structure. It is situated, however, upon the naked beach. The Union is the dike to fence out the flood. That dike is broken and decayed, and if we do not repair it, when the next spring-tide comes, we shall be buried in one common destruction."[53]

The images here are of powerful forces of nature that can be restrained only by well-planned cooperation. I suspect they are from Dutch history as much as British or New England, but their application is unmistakable. The natural state is not one to be desired. Nor even the tribal state. The liberty to be found there is forever in question—if the sword-arm fail. Yet human society is so frail a shelter as to be constantly threatened by the encroachments of depravity. Earlier in the convention Ames observes that people who talk about the "liberty of nature" make a "declamation" against matter of fact.[54] We are thus reminded not of John Locke but of Thomas Hobbes and of the repetitious misconduct of the seed of Abraham in the narrative sections of the Old Testament.

But perhaps just as eloquent as Ames's summary of the case for ratification is the one made by Jonathan Smith of Lanesborough, who, though pointedly rustic in his delivery and self-description, is as subtle in reasoning for adoption as any of the lawyers or clergy who are active in that cause. Smith urges the anxious Antifederalists to consider a case where two or three of their number "had been at pains to break up a piece of rough land, and sow it with wheat."[55] Then he asks them to suppose further that they could not agree on how to protect the crop. Only then does he ask, "Would it not be better to put up a fence that did not please everyone's fancy, rather than not fence it at all, or keep disputing about it, until the wild beasts came in and devoured it."[56]

General William Heath makes a speech to the same effect, using the old parable of the rebellion of the members of the body against the whole. He does not speak of commerce or profit but of union. What he and Smith and Ames and Parsons say is clearly the Federalist teaching on the value of union—and a measure of how different from the Constitution adopted in Virginia and New York, North and South Carolina was the theory of government affirmed by Massachusetts when by nineteen votes it ratified what the Framers had made.[57]

What we find in the record of the ratification conventions of the South and the middle states is an emphasis on the external objectives of government, the limits on what it attempts to achieve, and the economic and military advantages of a more perfect Union. According to these constructions, government is more a necessary evil than a positive good—or at least the government of the United States, as opposed to state and local governments. In these conventions the regnant myths of the American self, of the national future, are very different from that of New England. The agrarian vision of the South and the commercial dream of Philadelphia and New York did not presume that "the state and society were 'indivisible' or 'co-extensive.'" [58] From the time of the Mayflower Compact, Massachusetts could not separate the two. [59] Southern Federalists did not fear insurrection or imagine that democracy and deference toward the natural leaders of the community were incompatible. Rights for them were an inheritance proven in the Revolution. Neither did they emphasize the liberties that only government could guarantee—though many of them agreed with Fisher Ames that man was a social being and that his rights could not be usefully imagined in an aboriginal state. Southern Federalists promised to defend liberty by confining federal authority to those functions explicitly assigned to its sphere. So speak James Iredell and Charles Pinckney, his cousin General Charles Cotesworth Pinckney, and James Madison. The latter in June 1788 in Richmond defined a Constitution that predicted his subsequent struggles about the nature of government with the people of New England, arguing that "the powers of the general government" will be "exercised mostly in time of war" and "relate to external objects"; that "every thing not granted is reserved [to the states]." [60] For a national government designed to transform the society that it protects he made no brief. It is an irony that the Constitution Madison did so much to create has, through the alchemy of our national history, become more like the one approved in Massachusetts than the one he hoped to establish. To understand such developments, it is necessary to see both of these alternatives in the context where they first appeared, to realize that there were other possible understandings and to acknowledge the forces that made it likely that one view prevailed while the others sank beneath the waves, caught outside the breakwater when the inundation came.

5

Preserving the Birthright:
The Intention of South Carolina
in Adopting the United States Constitution

Each of the thirteen states that ratified the original Constitution of the United States produced its own versions or subdivisions of the Federalist and Antifederalist parties and its own discrete reasons for agreeing to a more "energetic" government according to terms specified in that document. Indeed, each of these states ratified a Constitution of its own, having persuaded itself to see its decision in a certain hopeful light, ignoring contrary implications of its action. From that multiplicity has followed a good deal of what has been dramatic about the political history of the Republic. The story of ratification in South Carolina and of the purposes of its leaders in securing that vote of approval on May 23, 1788, is a measure of the general proposition I have just announced, a case in point.

Rhode Island finally ratified (May 29, 1790) because, with Congress standing ready to punish its intransigence, it had no other choice. North Carolina faced the same sort of compulsion but also was influenced in the direction of assent by the good faith effort of the First Congress of the United States in offering the Bill of Rights for approval by the states. Georgia approved the Constitution because it could not defend itself, especially against the Creek Nation concentrated just west of its frontiers. New Jersey and Delaware agreed because they needed economic protection against New York and Pennsylvania: they could not function well as sovereign commonwealths, given their geographical situation, size, and resources. New York, with a large but ineffectual Antifederalist majority, ratified because Virginia had just done so—and for fear of its own internal divisions. Pennsylvania agreed early, Philadelphia having already developed a national spirit and an eye to the main chance. For these reasons and because James Wilson spoke so well of the fine things a stronger government might do or encourage. Moreover, like the city of New York, Philadelphia during and after the Revolution had been home to the Continental Congress and knew how it was injured by the government's inability to levy and collect a tax.

Connecticut thought like Massachusetts and most of New Hampshire—after Captain Shays's Rebellion. Roger Sherman and Oliver Ellsworth persuaded its local-minded citizens that the regime (and the life) which they cherished would not be threatened by union. New Hampshire also finally responded to what Massachusetts had done, and to an almost Antifederalist exposition of what the Constitution would mean. Even more than Virginia, Maryland was impressed by General Washington's support of the Constitution—by this one advocate, by reaction to local Antifederalist leadership, which had to do with local politics, and by the idea of a share in western lands turned over to the general government (also an influence over several other "landless" states).

More complicated instances of my proposition are to be found in Massachusetts and Virginia and South Carolina. I have already mentioned the foundation of Virginia Federalism—the very person of General Washington. That brand of Federalism was gone forever within just a few years of Washington's death. But perhaps almost as important in overcoming a profound uneasiness about some of the implications of the Constitution in Virginia's June 1788 convention was the narrow minimalist reading of its text made by Federalist speakers such as Henry Lee, John Marshall, Edmund Pendleton, George Nicholas, George Wythe, and the late convert to that cause, Edmund Randolph. That reading, orchestrated and detailed (almost personified) by James Madison, added to the fact that all Virginians realized they were expected to take the lead, that theirs was the largest state, theirs the natural role of leadership, and theirs the primary responsibility for the attempt to replace the Articles with the proposed Constitution.

With Massachusetts, the definitive reasons for final approval of the Constitution in its early ratification convention are more particular, exceptional, and indigenous to the unusual and self-conscious history and situation of that American Zion. And also more philosophical. It is important that Samuel Adams and John Hancock, for personal reasons, did not give themselves fully to the cause of Antifederalism and that many local magnates and leading men from outside of Boston, responding to Shays's Rebellion, took up the Federalist cause. But the most important explanation of Massachusetts's decision to ratify lies in the fact that it was the Puritan commonwealth, marked by 170 years of Puritan thought on the positive advantages of government as a source of human virtue, freedom, and felicity, resonant of a hundred artillery sermons and a thousand spiritual autobiographies.

These are admittedly simplistic accounts of complicated events, of motivations as uncertain and various as the populations that they summarize. But they are also, within their limitations, true—and most suggestive of how different the Constitution seemed to assorted imperceptive examiners living in the era of its origination. Different, even though all of the states recognized the need for a new constitution and saw the necessity embodied in the four purposes for a stronger general government detailed in Philadelphia by that mild and judicious Federalist from Connecticut, Roger Sherman. On Sherman's list of "objects of Union" were defense against invasion, control of internal disputes and disorders, treaties, and foreign commerce from which a revenue might be derived.[1] In these purposes and a few more the states were agreed.

*T*he ratification of the United States Constitution in South Carolina was as circumstantial and political as it had been, or was to be, in other states. It could be argued that South Carolina ratified the Constitution on May 12, 1780, the day Sir Henry Clinton marched into Charleston and occupied the city. In other words, South Carolina was resolved after this bitter experience to accept as fact that an absolute independence of the several states was an invitation to foreign invasion and had remembered the great lessons of military Federalism even when at peace, though it had discovered other reasons for ratification after independence had been achieved.

But it is perhaps best to begin consideration of what South Carolina intended by its decision to affirm the handiwork of the Great Convention by taking note of what it did not mean by that choice. The Constitution interpreted as a fundamental law that could but (in the view of many) should not be approved in Charleston is the subject of the sharpest exchanges in the legislative debates that authorized a ratification convention in the Palmetto State. General Charles Cotesworth Pinckney, Edward Rutledge, Charles Pinckney, John Julius Pringle, David Ramsay, Robert Barnwell, and John Rutledge argue against this reading of the Constitution and Rawlins Lowndes for it. These exchanges are negative proofs of South Carolina's purposes in finally agreeing to accept its place in the Union — and of how it finally understood the implications of that choice.

The first and most obvious conclusion that we may draw from the discussion of ratification in the South Carolina legislative sessions of January 16–19, 1788, is that the members of the assembly had no notion of voting for a constitution instrumental in its promotion of a lasting national commitment to philosophical abstractions: a constitution designed to translate anterior, universal rights into present policy. Charles Cotesworth Pinckney spoke plainly, to the common repugnance of his colleagues, toward the notion of such a version of fundamental law when he warned them against the danger of confusion and hypocrisy in insisting on a national "Bill of Rights."[2] To such an itemization he raised a number of objections: (1) the Framers thought it improper to mention specific rights guaranteed under state law "for, as we might perhaps have omitted the enumeration of some of our rights, it might hereafter be said we had delegated to the general government a power to take away such of our rights as we had not enumerated"; (2) they believed that silence on the subject of rights would keep the general government away from that potentially explosive subject — and away from endangering inherited rights otherwise made secure; (3) they realized that South Carolinians could take part in declarations concerning human rights only "with a very bad grace, when a large part of our property consists in men who are actually born slaves" —

and that the various bills of rights usually began by declaring that "all men are born free" or with similarly broad statements about human nature and destiny. That kind of addition to or inclusion in the Constitution General Pinckney knew to be unacceptable to his state. His argument was that no such instrument went out from Philadelphia. Rawlins Lowndes made just the opposite case.

The pleadings of the South Carolina Antifederalists against the Constitution as a potentially dangerous instrument were essentially the arguments of Rawlins Lowndes, the prophetic voice for a Southern conservatism that would emerge and dominate the region in the generation following his own. How fiercely they were maintained by Lowndes in the January legislative debates was demonstrated when he declared that he "wished for no other epitaph, than to have inscribed on his tomb, 'Here lies the man that opposed the Constitution, because it was ruinous to the liberty of America.'"[3] At sixty-eight, Lowndes was one of the recognized leaders of his society, a former president of South Carolina and an obvious spokesman for his state's sense of continuity with its English past, its uneasiness about too close a connection with its sister commonwealths north of Baltimore. There is an affinity between his sectionalism and that which Edward Rutledge expressed during the discussions that preceded South Carolina's approval of the Articles of Confederation.[4] We can detect an undercurrent of distaste for New England and all of its works, its "low cunning" and "levelling principles," such as we find in the correspondence of most of his state's leading figures.[5] Moreover, though Lowndes is not talking about just slavery when he warns against subjection to a Northern majority, he was in agreement with General Pinckney (and other Federalists who are presenting the Constitution for debate) that his people cannot live under a fundamental law that will not allow them to think of their "peculiar institution" as a "positive good" and to act upon that belief.

Concerning the importation of slaves to replace those stolen or lost during the Revolution, Lowndes argued that "this trade could be justified on the principles of religion, humanity, and justice; for certainly to translate a set of human beings from a bad country to a better was fulfilling every part of these principles." He attributed the Northerners' aversion to slavery to the fact that they had none themselves, and "want to exclude us from this great advantage."[6] Then he recalled General Pinckney's public position on why Southerners need slaves. In contending for the advantages of slavery for both bondsman and master, Lowndes goes the full distance — thus belying a commonplace of the scholarship, that Southerners made no more than a circumstantial case for slaveholding for another forty years.[7] But Lowndes's point was larger than the proslavery argument it subsumes, a warning against Northern "jealousy" and "encroachment": of how one restriction on the liberties of his neighbors (made, of course, for "good" cause) might lead to another, until "the interest of the Northern States would so predominate as to divest us of any pretension to the title of a republic" and allow them to do with South Carolina as they wished.[8] That is, until the local legislature had "dwindled down to the confined powers of a corporation."[9] To emphasize these dangers, he focused on the word "experiment" as it was employed by young Charles Pinckney in his narrative of the transactions of the Great Convention and defense of the positions taken by South Carolina's members of that worthy company — a report that opened these January debates and was designed to pacify Antifederalists.[10] Lowndes then expatiated on the negative implications to be discovered in the term.[11]

In observing the local Federalists worshiping the problematic beauties of the Constitution as if it were the "golden image" that so bemused the Jews in Exodus, Lowndes conjured up the dark future that such credulity might produce. By this meditation he is carried toward a warning against the danger of rash speculation to that larger "family" which is the community — a family supposedly represented by all those who hear him.[12] "It has been said that this new government was to be considered as an experiment. . . . An experiment! What, risk the loss of political existence on experiment! No sir; if we are to make experiments, rather let them be such as may do good, but which cannot possibly do any injury to us or our posterity."[13] By this formula the Federalists who confronted Lowndes in a "phalanx" were transformed into mere projectors, men careless with (or indifferent to) the means and welfare of those whose future was in their keeping.[14]

The Federalist response (apart from General Pinckney's forceful correction of Antifederalist ignorance of the law of treaties) was that the Constitution is a protection for South Carolina as it has been and hopes to be: a structure that staves off the dangers of anarchy and despotism.[15]

According to these Federalists strength in combination compensates for Southern weakness and is a source of freedom, not a danger to it.[16] The experimenting can only go so far because "it is admitted, on all hands, that the general government has no powers but what are expressly granted by the Constitution, and that all rights not expressed were reserved by the several states."[17] Or, as Charles Pinckney observed, "no powers could be executed, or assumed, but such as were expressly delegated."[18]

Specifically, the Federalists maintained that the new government "can never emancipate" the slaves, injure the commerce of South Carolina, or otherwise subjugate the region. Moreover, they were quick to add, the Yankees have been so kind as to grant Southerners a new power to recover their runaways—a power not available under the Articles. In any case, even if Northerners reverted to the bad attitudes toward their countrymen once expected of them, the South was the region that was growing and would soon be able to outvote them.[19]

Rawlins Lowndes was impressed by none of these observations. "Let us compare what we already possess," he suggested, "with what we are offered for it." From the behavior of Northern leaders in questions relating to the tariff, to the regulation of commerce or the slave trade, it was easy for him to infer "what we may expect in the future." The great merit of life under the Articles as opposed to the "proffered system" was that it provided safeguards against sectional exploitation. The "gentlemen who had signed the old Confederation were eminent for patriotism, virtue, and wisdom . . . in the care which they had taken sacredly to guaranty the sovereignty of each state."[20]

It was Lowndes's concern that in the proposed Constitution no such protections for self-government were provided, not even so much as Scotland retained when joined to England, or as were offered Americans by Lord North after the colonists proved difficult to subdue.[21] Concerning the prospective benevolence of "our kind friends to the north," Lowndes is sharply sarcastic. He is convinced that few Carolinians will believe General Pinckney's optimistic stories about Northern pliability and goodwill. New Englanders were "governed by prejudices and ideas extremely different from ours" and were not to be trusted politically under the provisions of the proposed Constitution.[22] The disproportionate burden carried by the South in fighting through the Revolution had made him suspicious.

"Some gentlemen had advanced a set of assertions to prove that the Eastern States had greatly suffered in the war. Pray, how had they suffered? Did they not draw from the Continental treasury large sums of money?"[23] Once the South is bound hand and foot by the chains of the Constitution, Lowndes foresaw what Yankee reaction to Southern complaints of unlimited Northern power would be. He supplied their side of the dialogue as follows: "Go: you are totally incapable of managing for yourselves. Go: mind your private affairs; trouble not yourselves with public concerns— 'Mind your business.'"[24]

Even at the remove of two hundred years it is easy to understand why Henry Laurens Pinckney, speaking on July 4, 1833, called him "the sagacious Lowndes." Though the old Antifederalist did not persuade the lowcountry to reject the Rutledge/Pinckney position and go with him, he was by no means "defeated" in his arguments with them, as all South Carolina admitted within a very few years. Over the generations, the Constitution became more or less what Lowndes had anticipated, containing as it did a potential for development in the direction of absolute power over citizen and state even when it first appeared: grounds for predicting as Lowndes had "that, when this new Constitution should be adopted, the sun of the Southern States would set, never to rise again."[25]

That is to say, anxieties about such development were well founded so long as what was said by the Federalists in the ratification conventions is ignored—their version of the Constitution that they intended as opposed to what it has become. And perhaps even when the local Federalists are not ignored. But forensic victory was not Lowndes's expectation. His primary purpose was to give pause, to require the Federalists to respond to his argument, and to get his and their readings of the Constitution on record. In this effort he was most successful, though as the local Jeremiah, he was, like his prototype, very little appreciated for the accuracy of his prophetic vision at the time he offered it.

From the May 1788 South Carolina ratification convention itself we have only fragments of the discussion—most of them echoing what had been said by Lowndes and his antagonists in the exchanges of the previous January. Here again the issue to be fought out is whether the Constitution would allow the general government to swell up into something much more ambitious than it appeared to be while being adopted. To complain of arbitrary impositions was not in 1776 to deny the Old Whig dream of a corporate life under the authority of a law both sovereign and limited in scope. To honor the example of that Revolution in the name of the South Carolina version of "the common and inalienable rights peculiar to Englishmen" was simply more of the same, though performed twelve years later. Delegates such as Rawlins Lowndes experienced "no love of innovation" in 1775–76—or in 1788. They found in "prescription and usage" the basis for law and "the best of titles."[26] But they had no patience with remote, hostile, or indifferent authority injecting itself where it did not belong. For in South Carolina the social bond, the links to the past, had not been broken by independence; and should not be, all Carolinians agreed, by the creation of "a more perfect Union."

Patrick Dollard, Antifederalist innkeeper, farmer, and justice of the peace from Prince Frederick's Parish, whose remarks are among the few speeches preserved from the ratification convention, summarizes this position when he insists that he is unwilling, even for the sake of temporary prosperity and national strength, to make over to "any set of men, their [South Carolina's] birthright, comprised in Magna Charta, which this new Constitution absolutely does."[27] Here is no claim to aboriginal rights, no appeal to philosophy or the justice known only in heaven. The doctrine invoked is less complicated. It is Dollard's teaching that his neighbors became Americans out of being South Carolinians, and were both because they belonged, even in 1788, to a particular Anglo-American identity not abrogated by the American Revolution. Moreover, according to Dollard's analysis of his state's reaction to the handiwork of the Great Convention, South Carolina would countenance no internal revolution through its final acceptance of the Constitution. By such men as Dollard, Lowndes, and Thomas Sumter South Carolina's purposes in ratifying were made clear and unmistakable. These opponents of too much government forced the South Carolina Federalists to offer assurances and situate themselves as men still living "inside the magic circle," even though they favored the Constitution by reason of its protection—favored it to secure the integrity of what we would now call society, as opposed to the state. In these matters the Carolinians thought like that ingenious apologist for Southern

Federalism, James Madison—as Patrick Henry had forced him to argue in the Virginia ratifying convention. They were not free, in Charleston or Richmond, to replace the continuity cherished by their neighbors by surrendering authority over their everyday lives to a power indifferent to or ignorant of their circumstances—not in 1776, and not in 1788.

The notion of a "birthright" of "inherited rights" coming down through a particular blood and history from 1215 and the Great Charter and preserved in a society that has never dissolved or surrendered its original identity receives a curious defense with reference to South Carolina. This defense of patrimony occurs after the Constitution had been ratified and the First Congress of the United States elected and gathered in New York. Its expositor is none other than James Madison, who in calling for acceptance of the credentials of William Loughton Smith to be a member of the House of Representatives from Charleston, outlines a theory of derivation of citizenship concerning the political order of the United States after independence had been declared and royal authority abrogated. Smith, a decided conservative, had been in school in England and Switzerland during and prior to the American Revolution but remained a member of his native community by way of his father and his other relations, through his guardians and his property. During the war Smith swore no oaths for either side. Having completed his education, he returned to South Carolina after the ratification of the treaty of peace. Yet Madison maintains that Smith is an American because his community did not break up and reassemble from a state of nature when it followed the example of English Whigs in 1688 and resisted the untoward innovations of a foolish prince. For the social and political bond that made South Carolina a self-governing, self-contained community following the creation of the colony survived intact after the Declaration of Independence: survived a separation from England within a larger Anglo-American political tradition and became then a contribution to the wholeness of the Union when South Carolina sent representatives to the Continental Congress and signed the Articles of Confederation. South Carolina, along with other colonies, withdrew from the British Empire with an antecedent integrity intact and took all those who were partners in it, in securing the self-preservation of a legitimate status, with it to live out something new within that tradition—but not in the spirit of "experiment." All of which is summarized in the person and history of William Loughton Smith,[28] who was not one to be included in a story about "wild experiments" or "feckless innovations."

Leaving aside the youthful eccentricity of Charles Pinckney (a prototype for generations of Southerners since his time who have hoped for a "national career"), South Carolina's delegates to the Great Convention got for their state most of the Constitution they had hoped for—a document favorable to the commercial life of Charleston, protective of slavery and necessary to the common defense. Indeed, the first complete draft of the Constitution was written by (or under the direction of) John Rutledge. Therefore they were able to answer Antifederalist objections to most of the particular provisions of the Constitution brought forward during its examination. But these delegates and their allies had to persuade representatives of a population that was, on the whole, indifferent or hostile toward the Constitution that it would not produce so many changes in the situation of South Carolina as to threaten the survival of the regime established there.[29] Whatever compromise South Carolinians had hammered out in Philadelphia with Northerners they could keep to themselves. Hence follows the symbolic conflict among versions of the document in question, readings of the Constitution as presented to them, in the local debates concerning ratification. The lowcountry magnates were obliged to embrace a contradiction before they could market it among the ordinary citizens of their state: to believe that they could enjoy the security that would come from language concerning "interstate commerce," what was "necessary and proper" to "the general welfare" and the "supreme law of the land," and not put in danger the special character of the South Carolina their forebears had made.

The dispute between Federalists and Antifederalists in South Carolina was really about how much in the way of fundamental law they could risk, not about the creation of a new order through the agency of a law that was instrumental in its character. Not all of South Carolina was easy with the text before General Thomas Sumter's motion on May 21 to adjourn the ratification convention until Virginia made up its mind. He had hoped that Patrick Henry might win the fight for him, or at least strengthen his hand with an impasse in Richmond. Disappointed in his original strategy,

General Sumter nevertheless was able to extract from the Federalists a statement attached to the record of ratification: "This Convention doth also declare that no Section or paragraph of the said Constitution warrants a Construction that the states do not retain every power not expressly relinquished by them and vested in the General Government of the Union." [30] As a codicil to ratification this passage was, of course, only the first stage in a long conflict, one that continues to this day. It must be fought out state by state, whenever we propose to alter the text of that supposedly mysterious embodiment of our sovereign will, the supreme law of the land. And fought out it should be, if we take seriously the doctrine that the intent of the lawgiver is the law.

6

A Great Refusal: The North Carolina Ratification Convention of 1788

Each of the ratification conventions with which the people of the thirteen original states passed judgment on the handiwork of the Great Convention had its own distinctive drama whose structural characteristics in the end colored the meaning of the Constitution in the communities by which it was originally approved. A focus on the multiplicity of complete ratification, once it had been finally achieved, has been a constant in my commentary on the process by which that compact acquired the force of law. Such multiplicity, however, is nowhere more evident than in the North Carolina Convention of July 1788 held in Hillsborough — not too far from Guilford Court House where, on March 14, 1781, General Nathanael Greene had faced down the best Lord Cornwallis had to throw in his direction. This convention, dominated by Antifederalists, voted 184 to 84 not to ratify the proposed bond of union as it stood when first presented to them.[1] Thus it said to the tide of history, "At least for the moment, no," and then sat back to watch the Federalist reaction to its refusal to oblige.

It was, of course, a foregone conclusion that the Hillsborough Convention was not going to approve the Constitution.[2] Willie Jones and his friends (Thomas Person, James McDowall, Judge Samuel Spencer, Timothy Bloodworth, and the Reverend David Caldwell) had done their work too thoroughly for any possibility of a Federalist "surprise" such as had occurred in New York. But the form to be taken by Antifederalist rejection was as yet undetermined, as was the use that might be made of the convention by the Federalist minority, a group of substantial citizens who were obliged to keep their minds on opportunities that might emerge if they handled their inevitable defeat in the most persuasive fashion.

The principal mistake made by the Antifederalists in connection with the first North Carolina ratification convention was that they delayed its meeting so far down the calendar of the ratifying process as to limit what they could achieve with their overwhelming majority—a delay of their state's approval until the Bill of Rights was adopted; or the scheduling of a second constitutional convention to amend the Philadelphia instrument, which had been suggested in New York as a means of recruiting support for ratification among equivocal Antifederalists. Had the Hillsborough Convention voted before Massachusetts in January or before the first New Hampshire convention adjourned on February 22, 1787, it might have released a tide of uneasiness and suspicion that would have brought Virginia, New York, and New Hampshire into the antifederal column: that would have sent Madison back to his drawing board and all of the Framers back to Philadelphia for a more certain clarification of the limits on what kinds of purposes might be achieved by the exercise of a proposed federal power.[3] But the delegates at the convention forfeited that opportunity by attempting to be too certain concerning the margin of their support in the Old North State and by trying to make the last play in the game, once everyone else's cards were on the table.

The blunder of the Federalists was in the opposite direction, in believing that North Carolina would agree without fierce opposition to a powerful bond of union such as its citizens had never contemplated while they moved toward independence. Even so, the envelope within which North Carolina made its choices favored the Federalists in the long run in that the people of the state wished to keep in place a connection with their countrymen in other American commonwealths; and because they were, therefore, sooner or later going to vote for ratification since, in July 1788, no other means were available to that fraternal end. Therefore, the strategy of the Federalists in the Hillsborough Convention was to make for the record a good case for approving the proposed Constitution and then to publish the apologia/transcript of those proceedings featuring the arguments of Archibald Maclaine, Governor Samuel Johnston, Richard Dobbs Spaight, General William Richardson Davie, and Judge James Iredell.

We are sometimes told that the surviving transcription of these proceedings underplays the participation of the Antifederalists and that Federalists edited it for effect. In a time when men were careful of their personal honor it is doubtful that Thomas Lloyd, Federalist transcriber, put words in the mouth of any Antifederalist. When the debates were published, too many important Carolinians remembered precisely what had been said. Hence I believe that there could be no politically significant distortion in the text as published—except perhaps for a little polishing of Federalist oratory to make it more attractive to Antifederalists they wished to recruit. For the historian of these events and the student of American political rhetoric, it is enough to know that at Hillsborough the Antifederalists "wanted only to vote": to know that the arguments made by Federalist orators were aimed at folk "out of doors," at those not present in the convention but potentially an influence in any subsequent assembly that might reexamine the subject of ratification.

N*o sooner did the Hillsborough Convention* come to order than it was invited to adjourn. On the general subject of whether the delegates would approve the Constitution, Willie Jones, having counted the house, moved the question.[4] In doing so he observed that delegates were certain to be familiar with the issues and the text of the Constitution, having had many months to consider their opinions on these subjects. Federalists raised an immediate hue and cry that such haste was unseemly and in conflict with the instructions that they had all received from the people of North Carolina to first consider and then to judge the instrument of government set before them. Jones shrugged his shoulders and behaved like the great gentleman that he was, agreeing to permit his neighbors to have the debate they wanted: to work their way through the text of the Constitution, section by section, even if Federalists had to put the case for both sides of many disputed points.[5]

This concessionary framework surrounding a conversation whose results were foreknown is part of the special rhetorical character of the North Carolina ratification debates. The other definitive ingredient present from the beginning of these deliberations was introduced immediately after Willie Jones's decision to allow a little Federalist oratory. What I refer to is the motion made by the Reverend David Caldwell: "Mr. President, the subject before us is of a complicated nature. In order to obviate the difficulty attending its discussion, I conceive that it will be necessary to lay down such rules or maxims as ought to be the fundamental principles of every free government: and after laying down such rules, to compare the Constitution with them, and see whether it has attended to them; for if it be not founded on such principles, it cannot be proper for our adoption." [6] In effect, what the Reverend Caldwell was doing with this motion was suggesting that the United States Constitution should itself be an embodiment of natural rights theory and of Whig teaching on the relationship between governors and the governed. The Reverend Caldwell would have preferred to live under a fundamental law dedicated to self-evident propositions about the nature and destiny of man, not according to a series of discrete provisions for conducting the work of government. What is most significant about the reaction of his colleagues to this motion that they draw up a generic statement on aboriginal rights to use in judging the Constitution is that they found it to be not only inconvenient and obfuscatory but also "dangerous": from "the nature of things" (in the phrase of Davie), unsuited to the business at hand, which it would delay or prevent and perhaps render impossible of resolution since delegates could never agree on such fundamental "principles" or "their application" (Davie again) and therefore would resist and/or reject whatever government that pretended to draw its primary authority from such abstract foundations. [7] The overwhelming majority (163 to 90) that rejected the Reverend Caldwell's motion was both a Federalist and an Antifederalist majority, reflecting the general sense of the people of North Carolina. [8] In their decision they recall the language of Edmund Randolph in the Great Convention when, on May 29, 1787, he introduced the Virginia plan with a contrast between the concern of the Framers with the problems of governance, with practical questions, and the very different preoccupations (with "human rights") among the authors of the Articles of Confederation. [9]

Given these predicates, the most important thing that can be said about the dramatic structure of the first North Carolina Convention is that, with reference to the strategy of the Federalists, it very much resembles all the other ratification debates for which we have records—or at least all but New York, where Hamilton was sometimes honest about the model of government under consideration. What I mean is, once they had dispensed with nonsensical objections to specific provisions in its text, Iredell and Davie, Governor Johnston and Archibald Maclaine all set out to identify the proposed Constitution with what the serious Antifederalists said they wanted, insisting at every stage in their discussions that the great fear of the Antifederalists, of a new model government that contained a potential for limitless expansion, was unfounded: that the first amendment suggested in North Carolina's recommended list, "That each state in the Union shall respectively retain every power, jurisdiction, and right, which is not by this Constitution delegated to the Congress of the United States, or to the departments of the federal government," was unnecessary since no implied powers existed and everything not granted by the states was "reserved" for their own administration.[10] In one exchange Judge Iredell declared that if the Constitution were subject to such expansion, then no one would oppose it more than he would: "No such wicked intention ought to be suffered." Efforts to annihilate the state government, "instead of exciting the admiration of any man, . . . ought to excite the resentment and execration."[11]

That North Carolina Antifederalism in its most important manifestations worried more about encroachment on the principles of local control and limited government than it did about the "rights of man" is, on the whole, better demonstrated by what the advocates of ratification in Hillsborough pleaded for the Constitution than by what its critics objected against it. Federalists understood very well what were (given the fierce Regulator localism of most Tarheel communities) the greatest fears of their neighbors. And these were not fears of Tory reaction or foreign invasion, not mere enthusiasm for paper money, suspension of debt, and mad democracy. In fact, very little had changed since 1766–71: since the Regulators had successfully identified local manifestations of the power of the general government in western North Carolina as an intrusive, ex-

ploitative, subjugating force. Schemes of overgovernment for purposes of
empire or to enforce a colonial policy not checked by local authority had
little local support—and seemed a surprising innovation. Such folk as these
Carolinians would not, in 1788, wish to introduce a remote, arbitrary, and
sometimes hostile power into their midst so soon after having expelled
such a power from their world.

Each state, insisted Judge Iredell, "must be left to the operation of its
own principles." [12] For as General Davie insisted, "There is no instance
that can be pointed out wherein the internal policy of the state can be
affected by the judiciary of the United States." [13] Nor could other branches
intrude where they do not belong. Iredell affirmed that "no power can be
exercised but what is expressly given." [14] And to the same effect Governor
Johnston maintained that any law made in conflict with the Constitution
would not be "an actual law." [15] And supporting this view, Archibald Maclaine thundered, "The general government cannot intermeddle with the
internal affairs of the state governments"—can "never intermeddle where
no [explicit] power is given." [16] Such was the central theme of the Federalists in Hillsborough—the right of their society within itself to persist in
its own chosen way, the commitment of the Constitution to that purpose.
The Antifederalists (*vide* Timothy Bloodworth) argued to the contrary that
the dangers were real, that "This Constitution, if adopted in its present
mode, must end in the subversion of our liberties." [17] And they pressed this
point fiercely, as if nothing else signified.

Of course, as the members of the North Carolina ratifying convention worked their way through the Constitution, not every provision of
the document drew them into discussion. Some Federalists complained
about the failure of their antagonists to make, once in the convention, the
criticisms of the proposed plan of government they had made in public,
in their communities. General Davie, "the great cannon of Halifax," expressed such irritation as the delegates began to comment on Article II,
Section 1: "I must express my astonishment at the precipitancy with which
we go through this business. Is it not highly improper to pass over in
silence any part of this Constitution which has been loudly objected to?" [18]
The other side of this exchange appears in the complaint of William Shep-
ard, that supporters of the Constitution were answering objections to it

which no one had made.[19] Yet despite the eagerness of their leaders to conclude the business and adjourn, Antifederalists did not sit silent. Indeed, the strategy of the Federalists to draw them out was employed with great success. Usually what the Antifederalists emphasized was their fear of creating a tyrannical power with legitimate authority over them.

While the Federalists spoke usually in measured tones, in quiet and reasonable exposition of the Constitution as offered for evaluation, the Antifederalists were full of warning and cries of alarm. Some of this coloring followed from their position, and some from their composite disposition. Their rhetoric is an instance of the classical *diaboli*, the warning of mischief to follow from a particular course of action. Federalists themselves employed this technique in insisting that the Antifederalists vote yes or prepare themselves for life "out of the Union."[20] Willie Jones answered their scare tactic with ease. He "had no apprehension that the other states would refuse to admit them into the Union, when they thought proper to come in."[21] And in no other way (leaving aside Maclaine's bad temper) is the Federalist rhetoric in this convention outrageous—as we would expect, given their ambition to reach and create a deliberate majority for the Constitution. Yet the Federalists were at their best not in measured exposition but in answering antifederal objections to the Constitution—especially when these gave them an opportunity to suggest that their adversaries did not understand the document. Looking at some of these objections in the sequence of their appearance at the Hillsborough Convention, I will illustrate in specific the Federalists' skillful use of "straw men."

First of all, there was an extended discussion of the provisions for impeachment that appear in the Constitution. Antifederalists took the language of these provisions as being open to loose construction. They were also fearful of being abused by the Congress if the House of Representatives chose to range widely and inquire into the misconduct of state officials or lesser public persons, or (as was more likely) that they might be denied relief from abuse by federal officers because of the remoteness of the authority that could review and punish such crimes in office. Moreover, they were interested in the procedure for having senators and members of the House of Representatives impeached before the end of their lawful terms. Governor Johnston asked of these enthusiasts for restriction,

"How could a man be removed from office who had no office?" [22] To this he adds, "Congress could not disqualify an officer of this state. . . . No body can disqualify, but that body which creates." To what his brother-in-law maintained Judge James Iredell added that a public officer should not be punished for mistakes or errors of judgment but only "if a man be a villain, and wilfully abuse his trust" — as with a bribe or acting to achieve some personal satisfaction. Iredell concluded, "A public officer ought not to act from a principle of fear." [23]

Some of the Antifederalists were not ready to hear plain sense on impeachment and were silenced with personal observations on their rational powers. Iredell upbraided them for refusing out of stubbornness to understand that only officers of the United States were subject to "the sole power of impeachment." [24] Other methods to secure redress of grievances against lesser officers of government were, they were assured, available under the ordinary forms of law. Indeed, one Antifederalist, James Taylor, spoke of how hard it would be to impeach a tax collector — and provoked an explosion of anger from that colorful and choleric Highlander and Federalist, Archibald Maclaine. This fierce partisan spoke of "wretched shifts" in argument and concluded, "I never heard, in my life, of such a silly objection." [25] Davie had earlier explained that impeachment in the Constitution "did not descend to petty offices." [26] But the Antifederalists, though rightfully and persuasively corrected, remained suspicious on this subject, as in other ways. They wanted to deprive the President of his exclusive military authority, to challenge the Vice-President's power of voting in cases of ties in the United States Senate, to remove the President's authority to vote on treaties, and much more.

Concerning federal control over place, time, and manner of federal elections, the antifederal objections were even more surprising. Once more, the problem was suspicion, the expectation that local elections would be stolen by federal manipulation. Federalists patiently explained the real purpose of these provisions of fundamental law. As Trenholme observes, the concern lurking behind these debates "was the fear of consolidation." [27] No less a man than Judge Samuel Spencer complained of the elections clause: "It apparently looks forward to a consolidation of the government of the United States, when the state legislatures may entirely decay away." [28] The problem of the Antifederalists in almost every case was that they could not imagine new powers for government apart from the prospect that they will be misused, or at least might be abused. Even Iredell at his most reasonable cannot allay this fear. The best argument that can be made for the Constitution in this connection comes from Governor Johnston: "States who have been as jealous of their liberties as any in the world have adopted it."[29]

Next the delegates turned to the subject of taxation. Even the most fervent Antifederalists agreed that the general government needed an enforceable power to lay and collect a tax. The existence of a mandatory provision in the taxing power was, therefore, not an occasion of dispute. But once again the Antifederalists saw in new power the prospect of subjugation. They preferred that no direct taxes should be levied on individuals unless the states were obdurate about collecting those requisitions that were their portion. Also they were alarmed that the absence of written limits on the power of direct taxation might, once these powers were exercised, leave the states with no source of revenue and drain away the very little specie circulating in their communities.

Taxes were not, however, the only financial issue to exercise the members of this ratification convention. A few Antifederalists, resentful of regulation, of proposed restraints on state action, stood up for the utility of paper money as sometimes less of an evil than the Constitution assumed it to be. They recalled its service in the struggle for independence. Governor Johnston replied with great force: the emission of state paper meant, in the end, theft by law. In North Carolina it had created a huge debt. Only fifty thousand pounds out of two hundred thousand had been repaid and hard money had been driven away. "Every man of property" in North Carolina knew better than to approve the practice.[30] Johnston's remarks on currency closed the money question. Antifederalists would have been satisfied on the subject had a few explicit safeguards against runaway taxation been provided. No issue had more to do with the existence of an antifederal majority in the Hillsborough Convention.

Sectional distrust and anxiety concerning the treaty-making power were other ingredients in the Antifederalist argument in North Carolina. When Joseph Taylor read the opening phrase of the Preamble he, for a variety of reasons, disliked what he found there. First of all, like Antifederalists throughout the country, he objected to the suggestion of consolidation and doubted that federalism as a principle could be reconciled to such language. But he also protested any inference that North Carolinians were really one people with the inhabitants of the North. "We see plainly that men who come from New England are different from us. They are ignorant of our situation; they do not know the state of our country. They cannot with safety legislate for us." [31] William Lancaster of Franklin speculated about whether the taxing power would be used by Northern majorities in the Congress to overburden Southern agriculture.[32] And his suspicions were not unique. William Porter of Rutherford County observed that a combination of Yankee senators with a Northern President might at any time revive the mischief of the 1786 Jay/Gardoqui negotiations and produce treaties that would cost the South dearly in lives and property through the closing of river traffic along its western frontier or the surrender of disputed lands.[33] In the same context, James Iredell, in discussing the language touching slavery in the Constitution, concluded by insisting that the document created no authority of any kind over the "peculiar institution," either in the present or any imaginable future.[34] All of which means that Iredell thought that Carolina Antifederalists had some anxieties about Northern attitudes on the subject. He added further that provisions in the Constitution for recovery of runaway slaves gave slaveholders a protection for their property that they had never enjoyed under the Articles or as colonials.[35] Iredell converted the reality of sectional feeling into an argument for ratification. But generally this material worked in the other direction. Indeed, as Richard Dobbs Spaight specified in warning against the costs of leaving North Carolina unrepresented in the Congress, tension between North and South was a given of the Hillsborough Convention.[36]

But the most important antifederal objections to the Constitution had to do with other questions not so regularly addressed in other state ratifying conventions as they were in North Carolina. These most serious criticisms concerned provisions for the judiciary and for the exclusion of religious tests from the qualifications for federal officeholders. More was said about the judiciary and religion in Hillsborough than in any other part of the ratifying process. Antifederalists argued that federal courts would obliterate the jurisdiction of state laws and judges. Moreover, federal justice would be both hard to reach and expensive. Samuel Spencer feared "clashing and animosities" between state and federal courts. Oaths of officeholders promising to uphold the Constitution he thought would eventually result in consolidation. And without a statement in the Constitution reserving to the states all powers not explicitly surrendered to federal authority, he wanted to see a bill of rights attached—one of the old kind that restrained Leviathan, not citizens or states.[37]

Though they agreed with Spaight that "no government can exist without a judiciary to enforce its laws," Antifederalists also objected to the supremacy clause because they were uncertain about how far it might reach.[38] Speaking for them concerning the provision for a federal judiciary in the Constitution, Timothy Bloodworth observed, "It is a total repeal of every act and constitution of the states. The judges are sworn to uphold it. It will produce an abolition of the state governments. Its sovereignty absolutely annihilates them."[39] Antifederalists also disliked the omission from the Philadelphia instrument of a provision for trial by jury in civil cases—even though Federalists gave them a good explanation of why it was impossible to do otherwise. North Carolina Antifederalists foresaw judicial imperialism far more clearly than their counterparts in the other states. In this particular, history has made them into prophets. Federalist responses to their objections to ratification also specified that these "friends of the Constitution" thought no better of lawmaking by the courts than their opponents did.[40] Speaking for them, Archibald Maclaine declared, "The federal court has jurisdiction only in some instances. There are many instances in which no court but the state courts can have any jurisdiction whatsoever, except where parties claim land under the grant of different states, or the subject of dispute arises under the Constitution itself. The state courts have exclusive jurisdiction over every other possible controversy that can arise between the inhabitants of their own states; nor can the federal courts intermeddle with such disputes, either originally or by appeal."[41] Maclaine so read the law, both because he wished it to be so and because he expected his adversaries to be satisfied by such a state of affairs, given their expressed preferences.

Concerning religion and the state, Antifederalists emphasized the secularizing and irreligious effects of a lack of tests for officeholders under Article VI. James Iredell's response to their concerns was the most distinguished and thoughtful of his many contributions to these North Carolina

debates. The people of the backcountry wanted no Anglican establishment, but neither did they wish to see the United States as less than an
openly Christian nation: a Protestant, Christian nation.[42] They did not expect to allow Roman Catholics into the highest offices. But, in particular,
they feared an influx of pagans, unbelievers, deists, and "Mahometans."
Henry Abbot, a Baptist elder from Anson, thought that such immigration
coupled with a treaty calling for the establishment of a "foreign" faith
might deprive the people of their religious freedom. For this reason Abbot
and his allies thought prohibition of religious tests of officeholders impoli-
tic.[43] What made the idea of such a treaty with a Roman Catholic power
plausible was the memory of an agreement between King Charles II of
England and Louis XIV of France, the Sun King—that memory, and a
network of old fears and resentments coming down from the Reformation.

Confronting these emotions, Judge Iredell drew upon British history
to demonstrate that nothing was implied in the exclusion of religious
tests but a hope of keeping the national government within the necessary
boundaries of restraint and away from the bad example of "establishment,"
British style. In his summary statement he declares, "Had Congress undertaken to guaranty religious freedom, or any particular species of it, they
would have had a pretence to interfere in a subject they have nothing to do
with."[44] The lack of a guarantee in the Constitution concerning freedom
of religion Iredell thus converted into a protection of such freedom—a
nice inversion of the case for a bill of rights. Furthermore, Antifederalists
were told that if North Carolinians could preserve a properly Christian
community among themselves, only Christians would choose to join with
them in moving into their state. Clearly, they did not wish to institute a
confessional state. But they were uncomfortable with change in matters
religious—as in all other matters. And especially with change engendered
by powers remote, unresponsive, and potentially unfriendly.

*W*ith *this series of questions* deployed and answered, the universe of discourse inhabited by members of the Hillsborough Convention is defined.
But the artificiality of this debate-for-the-record evaporated as it unfolded,
so that before Willie Jones—after a week of discussion and a conclusion

of the exchange on religion—moved the question, it had become a very serious discussion of the largest political issues involved in the choice for or against ratification. After listening to certain antifederal nonsense of what might happen, thanks to the existence of new powers, Judge Iredell declared, "Sir, it is impossible to treat such idle fears with any degree of gravity."[45] Judge Spencer supported him by declaring that "as there is not a religious test required, it leaves religion on the solid foundation of its own inherent validity, without any connection with temporal authority; and no kind of oppression can take place."[46] But in reacting to the overall thrust of the North Carolina ratification convention, Iredell also acknowledged that there were deeply felt and reasonable concerns underneath the entire Antifederalist argument—anxieties he was obliged to address because they reflected the loftiest of American political values, uncompromised by social or practical considerations. Speaking with admiration of the Antifederalist community that fought him all the way on ratification, Iredell affirmed, "I believe the passion for liberty is stronger in America than in any other country in the world."[47] The North Carolina Federalists, even though they had several objectives in reforming government that went beyond what was acceptable to their Antifederalist opponents, agreed with them about protecting liberty. Therefore, they responded to their announced concerns as well as the Constitution would allow, minimizing how strong a government ratification would make; attaching a reading to the document of no value to inventive modern judges. In other words, they understood far better than local-minded opponents that the "general ground of the objections seems to be, that the power proposed to the general government may be abused."[48] Such was the crux of the North Carolina ratifying convention.

For what the Federalists faced in Hillsborough, as some commentators on the event still fail to recognize, was the old Regulator spirit, a political temper absolutely unlike that of the Federalists.[49] The members of that majority had no patience with the idea of the teleocratic state, even if some version of union was, as they recognized, inevitable. For they knew, as Archibald Maclaine insisted before the entire convention, that it was "impossible for any man in his senses to think that we [North Carolinians] can exist by ourselves, separated from our sister states."[50] Even so,

North Carolina Antifederalists, in giving a vigorous rebuff to the idea of an instrumental state, set lasting limits on the meaning of the Constitution they did not yet approve. For North Carolina Federalists declared that their opponents were being offered just what they (ostensibly) desired. The Antifederalists thought otherwise.

Samuel Spencer, speaking for these reluctant Framers, said of the Constitution that "the state governments are not sufficiently secured, and that they may be swallowed up by the great mass of powers given to Congress."[51] William Goudy in the same cause declares that the disposition of the Constitution "to destroy the state governments, must be clear to every man of common understanding."[52] And there is more of the same sort of language from Timothy Bloodworth, the Reverend Caldwell, and others. In responding to such charges, Federalists found an agenda for their own political speech and were thus restrained from construing the Constitution as anything more ambitious than what the Antifederalists were saying they were ready to accept. Their rhetoric resembled that of the Virginia Federalists, just as the speech of their opponents calls up an image of the Virginia Antifederalists who were fully visible in the amendments to the Constitution proposed in Richmond and then proposed again in Hillsborough.

One of these suggested changes sent out to the other states by a recalcitrant North Carolina is, given the original rejection of the Reverend Caldwell's proposal that they begin with a declaration of rights, surprising. For such a list is recommended to the rest of the country along with North Carolina's "great refusal" to accept the plan of government proposed: recommended to the attention of the general government as a maxim to be considered in the framing of its laws and policies. And the list begins with a statement about "certain natural rights" of "men" and their "posterity" when "they form a social compact."[53] Making this statement all the more puzzling is the fact that North Carolinians had said nothing about human rights or equality in drawing up their original state constitution—a statement concerning the ground rules in their relations with one another.[54] But the contradiction here is only apparent: consistent with North Carolina's internal agreement on the subject of rights, its devotion to liberty and its fear of an indifferent, potentially hostile, or presumptuous national authority—of power not directly responsive to a local source.

The majority in the Hillsborough Convention did not change their minds on human rights in the course of their debates with Federalists. Vis-à-vis other North Carolinians, no such lever was needed for self-protection. Within the community where power was always restrained and responsive to popular resentment, discrete rights were enough. Antifederalists who wanted to keep a religious test for officeholders and (as in Virginia) to remain free to practice rough justice with bushwhackers were not, in the federal context, interested in regulating the conduct of citizens in their relations with one another—or, indeed, in having government protect their civil rights in their own communities.[55] The Antifederalist notion of rights had to do with restraints on the general government, preventing its intrusion into certain areas, but suggested nothing like our notion of civil rights as abstracted from our favorite misunderstanding of the Fourteenth Amendment. The Antifederalist notion of the rights of freemen united in society was a protection against the ostensible benevolence of a general government but useless in making positive reforms touching individuals or state governments, however well intentioned. Hence arises the provision in their proposed Declaration of Rights tracing the checks on the power of government all the way back to nature. In restraining the general government, such an appeal to the providentially given character of the world might be useful.

Talk of rights in the Hillsborough Convention meant that its members were agreed in making the value of limited government the fundamental premise of their exchanges. Even so good a Federalist as General Davie declared, "whatever might affect the states in their political capacity ought to be left to them."[56] The Bill of Rights, Antifederalists hoped, would protect citizenship in North Carolina from the danger of a federal definition. Contrary to Michael Lienesch, the antagonists debating ratification in North Carolina differed on how best to have state and local responsibility for personal rights, limited government, and sufficient federal power, not over whether these were worthwhile concerns.[57] With a Declaration of Rights restricting the notion of federal protection for positive rights, the old idea of corporate liberty survived among them.[58] But only so long as it was the general government that was restrained. The rest of the Union was thus forewarned by Carolina's united refusal to ratify that no expansive nonsense would be tolerated. At Hillsborough the perennial problem of American politics got a thorough hearing: the conviction that as a people we cannot live at ease either with or without a national government and therefore will be forever at odds about which side of this antithesis we should prefer to emphasize in our own time.

7

Religion and the Framers:
The Biographical Evidence

To understand the First Amendment to our Constitution as it stood before going out from the original Congress of the United States to be considered by the various commonwealths that in 1788 joined together in "a more perfect Union," it is necessary that we ignore the case of *Everson v. Board of Education* and what followed from that 1947 watershed decision — that is to say, necessary to work backward into the life of the early Republic and finally toward its English and colonial antecedents. For, in blocking us off from the record of history and the context of this lawgiving, the milieu to which its idiom belongs, the Everson case with its emphasis on Jefferson's "wall of separation" between religion and the political has confused the issue beyond recognition. Instead of rehearsing the errors of a desperately politicized Supreme Court, I propose to recover as dramatic present the human ground upon which the relation of general government to religion was, as the nation began, determined and the intellectual context within which the meaning of that resolution as crystalized in language can be known. By following this procedure we should be able to discover why the justices subsequently lost their way on the subject of religion and government and why they have, even now, such difficulty in finding a path that could lead them to a logical conclusion on this question — a basis for making up their minds as to which view of the Constitution to follow.

Part of the confusion that so often leads us to a misunderstanding of the original Constitution and Bill of Rights is the special status to which a selected group of early American leaders have been elevated as the quintessence of what the Founders had in mind in accomplishing our national independence and then channeling the impetus generated with the Revolution into the creation of a new form of government, one that is "part national and part federal." These few are forced to serve as heralds of a "golden moment" of "perfect toleration" and public enlightenment, the embodiments of reason, and are put forward as windows on the American soul, on the collective spirit from which, as a people and polity, we most legitimately derive. The difficulty with this tendentious interpretive strategy is that the student of early American history who goes to the trouble to learn about the private lives of a reasonable number of important public figures in the original thirteen states can discredit it with ease. The selective, disingenuous past visible when filtered through such a list is one well-calculated to foster a partisan misuse of the Constitution in rearranging the present. With the moderns and impenitent futurists who invoke this authority with reference to religion, the names thus collected are a constant: Thomas Jefferson, Thomas Paine, and Benjamin Franklin along with such lesser figures as Benjamin Rush and James Wilson. To this set it is conventional to add that part of Madison which seems to have a natural place in such company. Apart from Madison, none of these heroes is a recognizable Christian. And even about Madison there are certain doubts. The point is that by emphasizing as "representative men" the members of this elite group of deists and secularists, modern interpreters of the First Amendment are thereby released to ignore the distance between the still very English/Whig/prescriptive world of the Framers and the favorite political nostrums and simplifications of the contemporary intellectual community. To describe the Framers out of a larger body of evidence taken from the entire generation to which they belong—of the 150 to 200 principal Founders of the Republic—is to acquire another view of their composite character, especially with reference to the original American tradition concerning liberty, the state, and religion.

As I have come to know through my own work, the concept of the Framers as ordinary Christians, as members in good standing of the various Christian communions found in early America, is supported by the recorded patterns of their lives. What I propose in the way of a collective portrait draws upon evidence from the usually ignored 95 percent of that group—ignored because they are not precursors of the present dispensation in law, ethics, and public policy. The assumption that this majority was likely to agree to totally secular institutional arrangements in the very structure of American politics contradicts almost everything we know about human nature, as well as the most self-evident components of Christian teaching concerning the relation of the magistrate to the ultimate source of his authority in God. They could not be both practicing Christians of their time and the source of the High Court's present understanding of the establishment clause. Either these Framers were elaborate hypocrites in being Episcopalian, Congregationalist, Lutheran, Roman Catholic, Methodist, and Presbyterian or the justices are confused. Or, better still, they are pretending to be confused. But before going further let us examine the biographical evidence and only then ask what we may infer from it concerning religion and the origins of the Republic.

Of course, the most unmistakable Christian evidence of orthodoxy comes in references made by the Framers to Jesus Christ as Redeemer and Son of God. These are commonplace in their private papers, correspondence, and public remarks—and in the early records of their lives. As a sample of such piety we should include the *ars moriendi* as practiced by Patrick Henry and the parting admonitions preserved in the wills of John Jay and George Mason.[1] Henry made of his death a demonstration of his confidence in the promises of the Gospel. With it he proclaimed what he had written to his beloved sister Anne (Mrs. William Christian) in Kentucky once he learned of the death of her husband: "Perhaps I may never see you in this world. O may we meet in heaven, to which the merits of Jesus will carry those who love and serve him."[2] In the same spirit Henry declares in his will, "This is all the inheritance I can give to my dear family. The religion of Christ will give them one which will make them rich indeed."[3] This sort of witness appears in other parting admonitions from the dying to the living. John Jay of New York writes in his will, "Unto Him who is the author and giver of all good I render sincere and humble thanks for His merciful and unmerited blessings, and especially for our redemption and salvation by his beloved Son."[4] And unwaveringly orthodox George Mason of Virginia bids his children farewell by declaring, "My soul I resign into the hands of my Almighty Creator, whose tender mercy's are all over His works, who hateth nothing He hath made, and to the Justice and Wisdom of whose Dispensations I willingly and cheerfully submit, humbly hopeing . . . thro the merits of my blessed Savior for a remission of sins."[5]

Such declarations are so frequent in the papers of the Framers as to belie the now familiar theory that our Republic came into being in a moment of absolute tolerance, of religious neutrality *qua* indifference or deistic rationalism embraced by most of the leaders of England's erstwhile colonies in North America. And not all of this evidence is relegated to wills or very private documents. For an instance to the contrary I invite the reader to consider the proclamation written March 16, 1776, for the Continental Congress by the soon-to-be governor of New Jersey, General William Livingston—a very public document announcing a day of humiliation, fasting, and prayer on the following May 17. On this occasion Livingston declares his hopes that the American colonies now headed toward revolution may be filled with the spirit of "sincere repentance and amendment of life" and "a solemn sense of God's superintending providence so that "through the merits and mediation of Jesus Christ" they may obtain "pardon and forgiveness."[6] And there are many others who speak with the same explicitness of the promise of the Cross—though not always, as here, for the entire country.

Other varieties of unmistakable proof of Christian commitment appear in the acts and language of Framers who do not always speak directly of their Redeemer but who nonetheless behave as no deist would: who witness in some fashion to the vigor of their orthodoxy, most impressively in decisions that they make without undue calculation. Expressions of Christian hope are commonplace in the papers of the Framers. Edmund Pendleton of Virginia in summarizing his own life speaks of the agency of providence as many Framers do in remarking God's shaping influence on the good fortune of Americans in general. Pendleton, in reflecting on his own unlikely success as a young man without advantages who rose to a place of prominence, writes, "I have often contemplated it as a rare and extraordinary instance, and pathetically exclaimed, Not unto me! Not unto me, O Lord, but unto thy name, be the praise."[7] Pendleton fought complete disestablishment in Virginia, as did Patrick Henry, Richard Henry Lee, John Marshall—and George Washington.[8] So did Samuel Chase in Maryland, Caleb Strong and Theodore Sedgwick in Massachusetts, Roger Sherman and Oliver Ellsworth in Connecticut, Charles Cotesworth Pinckney in South Carolina, and many more.[9] Out of such pious evidence we must assume a widespread preference in their midst for a version of religious toleration not related to Jefferson's "wall of separation"—a doctrine that in an 1802 letter to certain Baptists in Danbury, Connecticut, he once advocated: a letter without legal significance.

The variety of surviving Christian witness in the papers and sayings of the Framers is indeed astonishing. Elias Boudinot of New Jersey was heavily involved in Christian missions and was the founder of the American Bible Society.[10] Roger Sherman wrote a sermon of "New Light" divinity and was a ruling elder of his church.[11] Richard Bassett rode joyfully with his former slaves to share in the enthusiasm of their singing on the way to Methodist camp meetings. Charles Cotesworth Pinckney of South Carolina set aside money to evangelize the slaves and teach them to read Holy Scripture. Pinckney had learned as a child "to love Christ and the church"[12] and distributed Bibles to blacks as president of the Charleston Bible Society. During the Revolution, Abraham Baldwin of Georgia served as chaplain in the American army. Earlier, he had been a tutor at Yale and in 1781 was offered the professorship of divinity there. Luther Martin declared with regularity his devotion to "the sacred truths of the Christian religion." John Dickinson of Delaware wrote persuasive letters to youthful friends concerning the authority of Scripture and the soundness of Christian evidences.[13] And both James Madison and Alexander Hamilton regularly led their households in the observance of family prayers. David Brearly of New Jersey and William Samuel Johnson of Connecticut devoted themselves to reorganizing the Episcopal Church in their states. John Witherspoon, erstwhile leader of the Scottish Kirk and president of the College of New Jersey, gave himself to the education of a Presbyterian clergy and to the composition of treatises such as "The Absolute Necessity of Salvation Through Christ." And William Few of Georgia was a lively frontier Methodist during most of his political career.

Such a catalog could be extended with private, casual, or indirect professions of Christian faith — as when Theodore Sedgwick of Massachusetts struggles to refute the charge that he is a deist; or when that conventional Episcopalian, Gouverneur Morris, writes his Tory mother, "There is one Comforter who weighs our Minutes and Numbers out our Days"; or when a dying Alexander Hamilton requests and after due penitence receives the sacrament from Episcopal Bishop Benjamin Moore.[14] Indeed, some of the Framers themselves, recognizing what people they bespoke, labored to extract from the Constitution proof that the new government itself and the nation that it served acknowledged God to be an authority over the regime, the source of all legitimate political power and the observing, supervising providence that will judge, as the returning master in the parable of the talents, the conduct of all magistrates and citizens. What I speak of here is evidence drawn specifically from the ratification debates.

Jonathan Elliot, in the second volume of his *The Debates of the Several State Conventions on the Adoption of the Federal Constitution*, records that Oliver Wolcott of Connecticut spoke against reinstatement of a religious test for federal officeholders by arguing that the provision made in the Constitution for swearing in of "the officers of the United States" made of such tests a pious redundancy. Concerning oaths he continues, "This is a direct appeal to that God who is the avenger of perjury. Such an appeal to him is a full acknowledgment of his being and providence."[15] Elsewhere, in the North Carolina convention, James Iredell argues very much to the same effect. The oath itself is a test, establishing that rightful political authority is inseparable from the acknowledgment of an ultimate source, flowing not from the people but from Him "who hath made us as we are," the Great Sovereign to whom we all shall owe an accounting for our stewardship in place. That oath is "a solemn appeal to the Supreme Being, for the truth of what is said, by a person who believes in the existence of a Supreme Being."[16]

Also inherent in the swearing of an oath are "rewards and punishments" for those who tell the truth or who lie about carrying out their responsibilities, regulation of the conduct of those in office — but nothing specific concerning their beliefs that might be connected with a particular religious commitment. In other words, only a little religion is being established with an oath—religion but not religions. Yet at times early Americans, when they speak of God's favor toward (or displeasure with) the nation, seem to treat their entire society as if it were a gathered church, one in its implicit covenant with the Deity. Such attitudes foreshadow (and validate) the quasi-religious Americanism of our subsequent national history and also the notion of a public orthodoxy with a serious religious content. The possibility of such a civil theology has existed since the August 15, 1789, debates on the First Amendment recorded in the first volume of the *Annals of Congress*.[17] It is not compatible with an absolute neutrality between belief and unbelief. It cannot coexist comfortably with the deists' notion of an impersonal God or with a universalism that denies that God makes distinctions between one people or group and another. Yet it is, with respect to the denominations, supportive of none of these communions in their exclusivity; and of all in those commitments that they share with the larger civil religion. Therefore it is also overtly hostile only to those religions that are absolutely exclusive in their demands for subservience and recognition from the state, that will not coexist with other versions of faith.

The Congressmen who, on September 25, 1789, voted out the twelve amendments (of which ten became the Bill of Rights) indicated precisely how much and how little they intended by the first amendment on their list to be approved by the states and did so by way of their use of the word "establishment"—a term with specific content as employed in Anglo-American political discourse at the end of the eighteenth century.[18] Concerning this section of the Bill of Rights we have from the United States Senate only the record of motions and revisions in language.[19] From the House of Representatives we have both that kind of information, certain letters from Madison and others, and the transcript prepared by Thomas Lloyd. But this evidence is more than enough to demonstrate that a neutrality tending to become a hostility toward religion—an instrument for secularizing the public life—was not the purpose of any participant in the process of this lawgiving.

When the amendment was first brought up for debate, Representative Peter Sylvester of New York objected to the Select Committee's version of an establishment clause since "it might be thought to have a tendency to abolish religion altogether." Congressman Benjamin Huntington, son of a distinguished governor of Connecticut, agreed with Sylvester, adding that because "the words might be taken in such latitude as to be extremely hurtful to the cause of religion," it would therefore be best that "the amendment be made in such a way as to secure the rights of religion, but not to patronize those who professed no religion at all." The language to which these legislators reacted specifies unmistakably the ground for their anxieties. It reads: "No religion shall be established by law, nor shall the equal rights of conscience be infringed." [20]

Moreover, the way in which James Madison, original author and promoter of the Bill of Rights, responded to Sylvester and Huntington (and to Roger Sherman, who wanted no amendment at all) indicates clearly that he took their objections to signify what I believe they meant: a fear that "no religion shall be established by law" would be read not as a prohibition of favor to particular religions but as a ban on religious activity per se, or on pious national self-definition of any kind; that this view would be reinforced if "rights of conscience" were construed to protect unbelief as well as particular sectarian commitments; and that both of these passages would do even more harm if the text could be interpreted as a prohibition of religious commitments by the states. Hence Madison responds agreeably to Sylvester and Huntington that he "believes that the people feared one sect might obtain a pre-eminence, or two [Congregational and Anglican] combine and establish a religion to which they would compel others to conform." A short time before, Madison had observed that "he apprehended the meaning of the words to be, that Congress should not establish a religion, and enforce the legal observation of it by law, nor compel men to worship God in any manner contrary to their conscience." [21] The key to these remarks is what all of these men understood by "establishment" and the difference between the first amendment in the form to which they protest and as it stands in the Constitution.

In finally providing, after much revision, that "Congress shall make no law respecting an establishment of religion, or prohibiting the free exercise thereof" the First Amendment ensures that federal action shall not prevent worship—prevent the chartering of churches within the states; and also makes certain that Congress shall not speak on the subject of a religious establishment. In this prohibition the language of the amendment carries with it an implicit acknowledgment of a truth recognized by the prescient James Iredell in the North Carolina ratification convention, where at one point he warned against including observations at law on the status of organized religion in the text of the Constitution itself. "Had Congress undertaken [in the proposed Constitution] to guaranty religious freedom, or any particular species of it, they would then have had a pretence to interfere in a subject they have nothing to do with." [22] And, after Iredell, a truth recognized also by Henry Marchant of Rhode Island who, in that state's ratification convention, on March 3, 1790, assuming that "this Constitution has no influence on the Laws of the States," maintained against James Sheldon of Richmond that "it will be dangerous" to call upon the new general government for a guarantee of religious freedom in the states.[23] For the power to guarantee turns quickly into a power to control. "Respecting an establishment" means "with reference to," not "working toward" an establishment, though the one construction presumes the other.

For the Framers of this amendment "establishment" was, with respect to religion, no mysterious term of art. The history of religion in colonial America, along with the record of religious conflict in England since the day of the Lollards, is presupposed in their use of the term. That much, but no more.

In 1789 a religious establishment was, in Anglo-American parlance, *sensu stricto*, an institution able (with the assistance of government) to promulgate a creed or dogma, to require official assent to that doctrine, to collect rates or some other tax in support of that religion, and to require, at least from time to time, attendance at worship. According to the limits of the definition, all religious activity not comprehended under this list of characteristics but encouraged or supported by the state or conducted under its auspices signified nothing concerning an establishment. Neither would the fact that a particular activity not sectarian in purpose happened to benefit one denomination more than another. In 1776 nine of the thirteen erstwhile colonies had, coming out of their colonial experience, something like an establishment by way of financial support for a particular church or combination of churches: continued so, though none of these taxes required creedal acquiescence to the faith of their beneficiaries or absolute uniformity in the patterns of worship allowed; remained thus probably because social conservatives were frightened by the idea of a government not sanctioned by "articles of faith."[24] By 1787 no full establishments existed in the former American colonies—nothing more than (in seven states) a kind of preference for certain species and combinations of religious activity expressed through public funding.[25] And by 1800 the meaning of the word had also been much attenuated in Great Britain—by purposefully lax administration of the Penal Laws, by the Indemnity Act, the Catholic Relief Act, the Dissenters Relief Act, and other measures coming down in a sequence from the great Toleration Act of 1689.[26] These shifts were part of the same development, in the end defining establishment as a few privileges and some financial support. Plural establishments, toward which many of the American states were inclined, were clearly a milder phenomenon than full establishment. Many religious conservatives, fearful of a decline in the churches (and thus in the character of the American people), tended to favor such a compromise.

James McClellan calls this tolerant arrangement "quasi-establishment." He concludes that "it would appear there were basically three patterns of church-state relations in late eighteenth-century America: quasi-establishment of a specific Protestant sect, as seen in most of New England; quasi-establishment of the Protestant religion, as seen throughout the nation; and the disestablishment of all religious sects as seen in Rhode Island and Virginia."[27] Working out of a recognizable historic experience that varied from state to state and responding to their own needs as free but religious men determined to reconcile the demands of liberty and piety, political leaders of the early Republic had, by the time the First Congress met, determined the relation of religion to government in their own communities. They wished therefore to be certain that these settlements, so successful in reflecting both their faith and their tolerance, rooted in the singularities of their distinctive colonial past, would not be disturbed by the adoption of the new Constitution.

Furthermore, knowing the history of religious conflict in their own commonwealths, in the United Kingdom and Europe, these leaders wished to preclude the repetition of sectarian animosity among Christians living on these shores, the kind of conflict that would ultimately undermine the status of religion among us. Though their perception is surprising to contemporary Americans who have benefited from two centuries of experience with inherited forms of toleration, these leaders thought there was a real danger of persecution. Designing men might tempt into a repressive alliance both Congregationalists and Episcopalians, and create a federally imposed establishment. They feared an arrangement like the one in the United Kingdom, with one religion established in Scotland, another in England and Wales. For they had been warned repeatedly of such a prospect, both before and during the American Revolution; and many of them were descended from the victims of religious oppression. Their voices, echoing such recollections, had been heard in the ratifying conventions. Yet clearly these anxious believers did not intend to be "extremely hurtful to the cause of religion" or to "abolish religion altogether" in order to perfect toleration. The focus of Madison's defense of the First Amendment to his colleagues in New York can be thus understood. It was a protection for citizens against a national establishment and, in the states, a protection of various quasi-establishments, not a threat to abolish them. Madison's original idea of making the amendment guarantee religious liberty in the states had been roundly rejected. By the time of the debates recorded in the *Annals*, he had accepted this decision. Therefore, even though the amendment precluded any action by Congress "respecting an establishment of religion," it left the general government free to sponsor all sorts of religious activity that said nothing of the possibility of a thoroughgoing "establishment," as that term has been used here. Madison's remarks in the First Congress about attempting to "compel men to worship God in any manner" or to "inforce . . . legal observation" says nothing against public prayer, support for church-related mission schools, or the Northwest Ordinance of 1787 with its provision of land to be set aside for churches. For as Madison recognized, his colleagues also seemed to agree, even as they precluded the creation of a national establishment, "that the Bill of Rights should not prevent the federal government from giving nondiscriminatory assistance to religion, as long as the assistance is incidental to the performance of a power delegated to the government." [28]

A demonstration that the amendment did not "erect a wall of separa-

tion" between religion and the government of the United States occurred
on the very day when it finally passed out of the Congress for transmission
to the states. For on September 25, 1789, Elias Boudinot of New Jersey
offered a resolution calling for "a joint committee of both Houses" of the
Congress to urge upon the President the propriety of a day of "public
prayer and thanksgiving." This language was adopted by an overwhelming
majority of the House. When debate followed this resolution, Thomas
Tudor Tucker of South Carolina objected (in a clear reference to what had
just been voted out as a revision of the nation's fundamental law), saying
that a Thanksgiving Day Proclamation was "a religious matter, and, as
such, is proscribed to us." Tucker had opposed the First Amendment. He
felt that to issue such injunctions went beyond the powers of the federal
government. But what signifies is not Tucker's purposes or those of his
South Carolina colleague Representative Aedanus Burke. Rather our attention must be on the responses made to them by the Congress. It was
brief and minimally respectful. Roger Sherman cited Holy Scripture and
Boudinot defended himself with precedents from the history of the Continental Congress. Then Tucker's fellow Congressmen answered his theory
about the First Amendment and the role of the federal government, responded by giving overwhelming support to Boudinot's resolution. Logic
insists, they could not have done so if the federal courts of today are correct in their talk of "a wall of separation." The rejection of the theory that
all religious matters are, for the Congress, proscribed is a reading of the
text on which that theory rested for its support — a reading of the authors
of that text. Those who say that the intent of the Framers in adopting the
First Amendment cannot be known are both intellectually dishonest and
absurd — disreputable in the way that ideology makes for what is shameful
in the arguments of men and women caught in its clutch.[29]

After reviewing the composite identity of the Framers as religious men
of a certain disposition, after remembering who and what they were and
the consonance of their collective character with what they did about religion and government, we are ready once more to confront the questions
with which this study began. What is sometimes lost in our reading of the
First Amendment is that serious Christians can travel only so far toward

that perfect toleration which prevents a public profession of faith in each and every circumstance, or which leaves God out of the performance of public duty, ignores His interest in and authority over our civil existence. To be absolutely tolerant is to be indifferent and less than fully Christian. There must be a point of tangency, as Saint Augustine maintained, between the City of Man and that more lasting habitation after which part of our nature yearns, wherever we reside and however we disguise our inclination. Therefore the ostensible neutrality of the Framers, the federal tolerance and horror of sectarianism that they made into a part of the Constitution, could not be allowed to become the kind of restriction on local religious self-expression that the idea of a wall of separation would require—or at least would seem to do so if certain language concerning "due process of law" in the Fourteenth Amendment could be said to incorporate the First Amendment. Clearly, as late as 1875, with the authors of the Fourteenth Amendment still in the Congress or active in the nation's political life, and the proposal of the so-called "Blaine Amendment" (providing that no state should "make any law respecting an establishment of religion") rejected, no such theory of incorporation was asserted by either the supporters or the opponents of expanding the commitment in the First Amendment to cover the states. There could be no point in such a measure if the states were covered already.

Once we have considered the first 150 years of our nation's legal history, we can recognize in its handling of religion a reflection, an extension, of the composite or summary Framer whom I earlier described as a conventional Christian and a social conservative.[30] In the successful effort made by that paternal figure to protect an arrangement already in place in 1789, adding to it the prospect of a nonsectarian national religious expression, we see fulfillment of the promise summarized in Washington's "Proclamation: A National Thanksgiving" of October 3, 1789: an acknowledgment that God deals with nations as well as men; that nations may pray, supplicate and give thanks, be pardoned, enjoy protection and favor, or endure deserved condemnation; a recognition that God may interpose, that He is the author of all good "that was, that is, or that will be." President Washington asks for his country peace, civil and religious liberty, the means of acquiring and diffusing "useful knowledge" — and as much prosperity "as He alone knows to be best."[31] He marks himself with all of this language as a Christian magistrate, enforcing legitimate laws that have divine sanction, even though they may only approximate pure justice. That he often employs periphrasis in speaking of the Deity signifies only a desire to avoid the appearance of sectarian assertion.

A nation that thus expressed itself might also invoke God as arbiter of great disputes, and judge of our individual behavior as social creatures in the City of Man. Such a country might proclaim His goodness as the measure of all that they admired and praise His name — while still refusing to commit itself to any sectarian particularities. But it could not confuse freedom of religion with freedom from religion. For as Stephen Botein has insisted, interference with "official religiosity at the state level" was (despite Madison's mistake on the subject) in 1787 "unthinkable." To this he adds of the Framers that "preponderant opinion, also coming from diverse sources, favored some provisions of written fundamental law that acknowledged public office and government generally to be under or of God."[32] The First Amendment in no way conflicted with this consensus. For it allowed the Christian in American public life to make profession by acting politically — to acknowledge that all government is of God, and under His authority — something the Christian must do if he is to live out, embody, the tenets of his faith. In this matter no neutrality is permitted, though the forms of profession may vary.

Thomas S. Curry, who has written instructively of the legal basis for religious life in colonial America, is clearly mistaken in maintaining that after the adoption of the First Amendment Americans did not understand what the new law required of them when they appointed chaplains, authorized Protestant and Catholic missions to "civilize" the Indians, and inscribed on the coinage "In God We Trust."[33] In 1789 they had made precisely the amendment they wanted and then interpreted that intention, embodied in that amendment, by what they attempted under its auspices — what they believed it allowed. We could not expect them as Christian statesmen to design a country that would, by reason of a "wall of separation," become an absolutely secular state: a country that, because of the provisions of the law, would not allow the federal legislature to express its purposes in terms of nonsectarian piety. They could anticipate that without fierce opposition some people might very well expend themselves in seeking greater and greater perfections of toleration—perfections that would, in the end, bring antireligious regimentation. As Christians, they (and their neighbors) recognized that something better (and more representative) than absolute toleration was necessary.

In conclusion, we may reason from the overwhelming biographical evidence and from the important texts which attach to it as personal or collective proof of motivation that, from what we know of the Framers (and of the three generations of Americans who followed after them) it is a farfetched conjecture to say that, through a series of gestures toward an ever more thoroughgoing neutrality, they set out to secularize America. To argue thus concerning the heritage that, of a purpose, they left to their children and grandchildren is to attribute to them what is not in human nature—indeed, what is contrary to that given about which we announce our opinions when we do not believe a character in a play or doubt a newspaper report of implausible activity. For, in so far as they held to a Christian faith, they would not wish to live in a society that in no way identifies itself as a Christian community, which in its impious political character would invite the wrath of God. Neither did they wish to put their descendants in a situation where they cannot profess their Christianity in and through their work.

Concerning the First Amendment there is still some good historical jurisprudence coming from the High Court, as in Chief Justice Berger's majority opinion in *Marsh v. Chambers*, 103 U.S. 3330 (1983). Such work should be acknowledged. It has kept the door open for a return to sanity. However, there can be no trustworthy standard for constitutional truth (no law per se) until the dishonest doctrine of incorporation is absolutely overturned and most of the Supreme Court's decisions touching religion made since 1940 reversed or revised on the basis of such evidence as has been examined in these remarks—in particular, the human, biographical evidence that could in the future serve as a decent restraint on judicial ingenuity and anachronism. Whether the still religious (and predominately

Christian) people of the United States have the strength of will to insist on such a correction is another question—one that must be answered politically in the process which results in the appointment of the federal judiciary at all levels of authority. Recently we have seen evidence that some such determination is at work.[34]

8

Changed Only a Little:
The Reconstruction Amendments
and the Nomocratic Constitution of 1787

Apart from the drastic revisions by tendentious construction and wishful thinking that have through Court or Congress attenuated our understanding and experience of the Constitution since 1932, there has been only one other period in the course of American legal history that threatened to alter, not by particulars but by kind, the nature of the compact that makes us, though many, in some sense one people.[1] I speak now of the decade that followed the conclusion of the War Between the States. And in particular of the first five years of that decade, when, with the South excluded from representation in a Union it had struggled to escape, the so-called Reconstruction amendments were added to the fundamental law of the land: amendments to which, before 1876, several civil rights laws were attached. In the fifty years that followed the adoption of these amendments and the passage of these laws a coherent body of judicial interpretation gathered around their combination and determined their relation to the old antebellum Constitution as it stood when Chief Justice Roger B. Taney presided over its application in the several sovereign states.

In general, I believe that these early interpretations were, in their cumulative effects, sound. They reflect a realistic understanding of the political and circumstantial limits faced by the lawgivers who made these momentous changes, both amendments and laws, a clear sense of their intentions, their piety toward federalism per se and therefore of their compatibility with a regime that had, before 1861, enjoyed what political philosopher Michael Oakeshott identifies as "nomocratic government": one characterized not by its objectives but by its mode of operation and devotion to a body of laws which codified that mode. These after-the-fact readings of constitutional history vintage 1865–75 presupposed also an antecedent Framers' Constitution defined by procedures, by a way of conducting official business, as opposed to a high-minded set of purposes hidden away beneath its surface like a ticking bomb.[2]

Received contemporary doctrine concerning what constitutes a proper regime defines a legitimate fundamental law for this or any other land by way of an ultimate substantive goal to be fulfilled by government in the translation from theory to practice of certain normative assumptions about the nature and destiny of man. To convert these assumptions into a mandate for policy and a discipline to restrain the misuse of personal liberty is, according to this view, the task of a true constitution. Such law, aspiring to fulfill such laudable ambitions, looks beyond uniform application, acceptable origins, and clear implications to justify its authority. And of other kinds we rarely speak. We have, therefore, for the most part, forgotten how to understand any other measure of established constitutional arrangements. To interpret the constitutional history of the United States we must remedy this lack, correct this provincialism in time, learn to see the world in the light of assumptions very different from now fashionable opinion. For our world's views in this connection are not the views of the Framers—or even of the Republican leaders of Congress in 1865–70, in the moment of the greatest radical influence on their behavior.

Despite the alteration that they made in the balance of American federalism, the Reconstruction amendments and early civil rights laws did not change the Constitution of the United States into a teleocratic instrument: a law with endlessly unfolding implications in the area of personal rights. On the evidence of history I must so maintain even though we have, as a people, chosen to pretend that they did produce such a change—did in fact, with anachronistic anticipation of some sacred inevitability, move the Constitution toward a conformity with the favorite political assumptions of *our* era: toward conformity with those assumptions, and away from the inhibitions of a division of power that made it difficult to scale such lofty reaches of doctrinaire "purity"; everlasting commitments in whose name they had fought a terrible war against other Americans perhaps devoted even more than they were to "the old teaching of the Fathers." These calculated misadventures in pretense and presentism, self-serving lies about an authoritative past (one that still has a powerful influence over our nation's affairs), tell us more about our current values and presumptions, our well-intentioned "lawlessness," than they do about the law itself—the merits and demerits of a Constitution that is, for the highest reasons imaginable, immune to pleadings in behalf of a justice outside its limits and cognizant of the difference between legitimate and illegitimate attempts to reconcile the one to the other—that justice and those limits.

To be sure, the minimalist view of the Framers' Constitution here advanced is not reflective of an uncontested consensus on that subject. Neither is it a unique and personal achievement—though the way in which I support it may carry something of a signature. But because I have another objective in these remarks, there is no place in this context for a detailed recapitulation of my reading of the Great Convention and of the following (and authoritative) state ratification conventions. Instead I simply assume as a premise of my argument the conclusion of Philip B. Kurland that the "public policy expressed" in the Constitution "is essentially procedural rather than substantive": that "almost all of the Constitution is procedural and not substantive in nature." Moreover, I agree with Kurland that most of the "substantive constitutional commands" that fill the United States Supreme Court Reports are "inventions or concoctions" of the High Court "rather than commands of the Constitution" itself.[3] I also share with Russell Kirk the conviction that "the Constitution is not a theoretical document": that its "foundations" are in "historical experience," practical choice, "religious convictions," conventional political practice (in the earliest American history), and a few contemporary writings.[4] And I also concur with Willmoore Kendall and George Carey about the distance between the Constitution and the simplistic understanding of the second paragraph in the Declaration of Independence.[5] Forrest McDonald wisely

concludes his masterful discussion of the intellectual origins and content
of the Constitution by emphasizing the difference between a fundamental
law that attempts to reform and reconstitute the society which it serves,
which is animated by a "spirit of system," and the kind of law that does
no more than protect and institutionalize a known if imperfect felicity.[6]
After 1865 the radical Republicans announced that they would attempt to
inject what McDonald speaks of as "first principles" and "higher values"
into a Constitution meant by the Framers to give them only "government
of the sort to which they were accustomed."[7] Which was, of course, for
Senator Charles Sumner and his friends, to admit that such "principles"
and "values" were imperfectly realized in the Constitution and laws as they
stood after Appomattox. Indeed, the radical Republicans constantly complained of such imperfection. It is therefore especially significant to notice
that they were, in the name of the more modest set of purposes contained
in the Preamble, successfully resisted by individuals who doubted that
such proposals could be reconciled to the American tradition of limited
constitutional government.

To proceed with my argument against exaggerated views of one segment of our national history it is also necessary to posit the idiom from
political philosophy, the universe of discourse, which it presupposes. The
case that I make assumes a basis for preferring one constitutional arrangement to another, and one method for creating law over any imaginable
alternative. Among its other purposes, this chapter is an exercise in making
distinctions about constitutional government. As I said earlier, much of
its framework (and some of its language) is drawn from the full teaching
of the British political philosopher Michael Oakeshott, not from just the
theoretical discussion of various kinds of political organization contained
in Oakeshott's memorable *On Human Conduct* and the related essay "Talking Politics."[8] For it depends also on his analysis of the formal character
of law as opposed to other varieties of human association in "The Rule
of Law," a chapter in *On History and Other Essays*.[9] What I maintain with
reference to the tenuous and ultimately illegitimate character of contemporary judge-made constitutional law is that it is an invention *ex nihilo*, and
thus an offense against the common good. The norm which requires that

even the best extrinsic standard of justice (*jus*) not be invoked to replace either the moral genius of a whole people as gathered in their history (*mos majorum*) or the "mode of human association in terms of the recognition of the authority or authenticity of enacted laws they prescribe" is *lex* as an end in itself, *lex* as a "non-instrumental rule." [10] It "cannot be identified with the successful provision of . . . substantive benefits" for any person or group but is instead distinguished by being made according to a certain prescription that is part of the law itself: "in which the jurisdiction of the law is itself a matter of law" — and also the way in which "law regulates its own creation." [11]

According to Oakeshott, the conventional modern state is (or pretends to be) an "enterprise association" whose nature is not defined by a civil practice, a common *way*, but by a civil theology. It is a *universitas*, which tends to be all-absorbing of those well-marshaled citizens whose lives it contains, and to see in them not persons but instruments. The older version of the state as *societas* was a regime in which society (as something antecedent and mindful of the person) encompassed the state. It is a structure that relates people "in terms of a practice" which, by the fact of their communion, they are morally obligated to observe. The *universitas* thus defined is teleocratic and the *societas* is a mesh of intermediate institutions under a prescriptive law "discovered" over time (values generated in context where being is logically prior to meaning), a *nomocratic* arrangement. The notion of law as a translation into statute of some anterior, universal truth abstracted philosophically from a particular view of humankind and/or God is what Oakeshott calls *jus*. In its unalloyed form as a "higher law," denying authenticity to all law not reaching its level of general truth, it belongs to the teleocratic state. [12] The older form of law that is marked by its origins and broad acceptance, reflective of how a particular people understand themselves, is merely *lex*, and is the backbone of nomocratic orders, elements of which still survive. [13] The value of the analysis that follows this exordium will derive from its testing of Oakeshott's interesting categories, both in politics and in law, against a segment of our nation's history and from asking what pattern in that history instructive to students of the United States Constitution is discovered through such an application.

Seen in this way, through this particular glass, what is the significance of the Reconstruction amendments and attached laws to our understanding of the meaning of the Constitution as a whole?

The evidence under consideration here must be organized according to chronology and apprehended in the context in which it occurred as a sequence, an order in time as well as in causality. There is no interpreting the Reconstruction amendments and attendant civil rights legislation of 1866, 1870, 1871, and 1875 apart from the political circumstances that made them possible, encouraged their adoption, and yet restricted how far they might reach in establishing a comprehensive federal protection for the civil rights of American citizens—rights of the sort traditionally reserved for definition by state laws, courts, and political processes, or for determination in unregulated private exchange.[14] It should be a given of any study of this evidence that the Republican leadership in all of these Reconstruction initiatives could not go too far beyond what its electorate would approve. Contemporaries cannot ask us to believe in a thing not to be found in nature—in the principled political suicide for causes not generally recognized as noble by a group of very ordinary, usually mendacious, politicians. They must read their history with more modesty. So long as these measures could be described as punishments or reforms imposed on the still rebellious South, they won grudging support, even in those areas of the North not too progressive in their attitude toward the blacks. But once they appeared as no more than efforts to improve the condition of blacks—as that *and nothing more*—much of that support evaporated. Soon thereafter the Reconstruction was at an end, with the Supreme Court as party to its conclusion. There were, of course, radical Republicans who favored all of these reforms on their merits alone—who wished to see them achieve something like a transformation in the status of the freedmen. Other Republicans hoped they would produce black votes without forfeiting the votes of Northern white electors. Some Northern jurists and legal scholars seriously hoped to see blacks uplifted, but not at the expense of the Constitution.[15] Democrats were in general simply opposed. Therefore the authors and apologists of and for these bills and amendments were obliged to present them as part of the struggle with Southern (and Democratic) wickedness, as stemming from the great moral drama of the war, without suggesting that they would much change the Constitution or alter beyond recognition the way blacks lived in New Jersey, Pennsylvania, New York, and the Midwest—indeed, everywhere but Massachusetts and a few other places. These are precisely the political realities that Lincoln faced in authorizing emancipation, and even earlier in debating Stephen Douglas. They are realities that defined the rhetorical and tactical problem of the Republican Party from the moment of its birth until 1883. The difficulty was to reconstruct, tame, and use the South without reconstructing Illinois, Indiana, and Ohio. It continues to be a difficult trick—no legitimate means of performing it being available, though during and immediately after the conclusion of a civil war, it seemed possible that there was a way.[16] Once egalitarian enthusiasm had diminished and devotion to federalism revived in the North, the optimism of 1866 disappeared—just as one would expect. In that atmosphere sensible men gave to the era of reform just concluded the disinterested reading that it required and after one hundred years under its authority in 1887 found the United States Constitution to be "changed only a little" from what it had been in the beginning: to be more a protection for a viable, functioning civilization than a blueprint to foster or require a social and/or political perfection not mentioned in its text.

There is a thematic advantage as well as a temporal necessity in beginning this analysis with the Thirteenth Amendment, for all of the politically motivated distortions of the record that have had an influence on the interpretation of these amendments and laws have their *fons et origo* in outrageous readings of the deliberate "national" decision to forbid slavery and involuntary servitude, to embody in the fundamental law of the land that part of the significance of the War Between the States. But the free interpretation of the amendment abolishing slavery is not only a model of later adventures in imaginative inflation of simple passages in the Constitution. It is also, ironically, a continuation of the arrogant, wrongheaded, self-righteous, and essentially "lawless" tradition of abolitionist historiography—often at its worst in dealing with the origins and meaning of the United States Constitution.[17] The reason we do not always recognize this strain of organized ignorance and effrontery in the writing of our collective legal history is that, after more than 100 years, it is still with us—still busy enlarging the scope of government, undermining the authority of the Constitution, and "freeing the slaves" by misrepresenting that record, distorting the significance of its particulars.[18] Of such trampling out of "the grapes of wrath" there is to be apparently no end. Or at least not so long as there is any power to be transferred by the exercise—or any sense of moral superiority to be satisfied.

It is of course to be expected that apologists for the going order or advocates of drastic change will attempt to shape that portion of history which is relevant to present questions into a sanction or precedent for their position on such matters: into an *argumentum ad vericundiam*, from accepted traditional values. Even so, abolitionist historiography, past and present, has a real problem with the Framers of this amendment. The favorite ploy of their scholarship is to make a positive proof out of the absence of evidence: to argue *sub silentio*.[19] According to this procedure the Thirteenth Amendment was intended to make of former slaves the equals of white men in both opportunity and condition—to abolish the erstwhile consequences of slavery while doing away with the practice itself. In this case the trouble with such a maneuver is that too much is known about the circumstances surrounding the approval by Congress of this change in the Constitution: about what radical Republicans attempted to attach to it and about how they were forestalled. Furthermore, we have an authoritative reading of the Thirteenth Amendment in two other amendments and assorted laws that were approved after its adoption, thus implying the absence of certain specific properties—what it did not mean.

Apart from all that its authors didn't say about the Thirteenth Amendment and its "larger implications" (and from what contemporary abolitionists and radical Republicans attempted to make of it even from the first), there is enough positive evidence of its original meaning to satisfy any reasonable inquiry. To begin, there is the reaction of his fellow senators to the attempt by Charles Sumner of Massachusetts, the master spirit of abolitionist doublethink, to attach expansive interpretive statements and language from the French Revolution to the plain text borrowed from the Northwest Ordinance of 1787.[20] According to Senator John B. Henderson, who presented this measure from the Judiciary Committee to the rest of the Upper Chamber, "We give him [the slave] no right except his freedom, and leave the rest to the states."[21] Henderson was from Missouri. Without him and others like him — Democrats and conservative Republicans — there would have been no amendment.[22] And it was politically impossible for them to support Charles Sumner's suggestion. Jacob M. Howard of Michigan, who was more interested in sending an amendment out for adoption than in incorporating the Declaration of Independence into the Constitution or applying the Bill of Rights to the states, urged his colleague from Zion to desist: "to dismiss all references to French constitutions or French codes" and turn back to more modest "Anglo-Saxon language" with the purpose of merely freeing the slaves.[23] Sumner later (1871) attempted once more to extract civil rights laws from the Thirteenth Amendment, even though he knew better than the rest of the Congress that this was a palpable violation of the Framers' intentions, as enforced upon him in 1865. The Senate had explicitly refused to say that they were making the freedmen the equal of other citizens "before the law." Senator Lot M. Morrill of Maine treated Sumner's broad-gauged derivation of authority with well-earned scorn and was in this attitude followed by both House and Senate. He challenged Sumner to discover such meanings in the text itself, with no talk of penumbras. Confounded and temporarily silenced by Morrill's challenge, Sumner, says his biographer, "discovered authorization in the Sermon on the Mount and the Declaration of Independence, for which he again claimed 'a higher power than the Constitution, being earlier in time, loftier, more sublime in character and principle.'"[24] This argument will serve very nicely as an introduction to abolitionist, teleocratic historiography but will not teach us anything about the Thirteenth Amendment except what it does not mean, and how it did not change the Constitution.

It is of course possible to belabor at some length what assorted ideologues following Sumner said in misconstruction of this amendment and then to refute them repetitiously.[25] It suffices for the purposes of this discussion to say that such repetitions would be mere overkill (acts of supererogation) and that it better serves us to understand how the specific prohibitions of this amendment relate to language already in the original Constitution — also prohibitions, but not general commands to achieve any specific, positive result: such as voting, the acquisition of property, or the right to do business with persons who do not care to do business with you. Which is to say nothing about the right to a particular place or standing in (or access to) society. It may reasonably be argued that the abolition of slavery would have been meaningless without the narrow protections of the 1866 Civil Rights Act—a law that offered no more (said its authors) than a right to contract, sue, take and dispose of property, give evidence, bring actions, and move about. Yet what appears in the amendment, even as implemented in the enabling legislation, is no more inclusive than the passage in the old Constitution (Article I, Section 9) that prevents the granting of titles of nobility by the United States and the reception of "Emoluments, Offices or Titles of any kind whatever from any King, Prince, or Foreign State" by any citizen of this country—unless he or she has the "Consent of Congress" to receive such honors— and also like another provision in the same Article of the Constitution that precludes preference of one American port over another by official acts of governmental favoritism. Both provisions are in the negative, both guard against some form of unearned advantage, and both are discrete— containing no appeal to general principle. In logic it is impossible to extract a positive mandate for equality out of three such negatives, for many other types of unearned advantage are left untouched by the Constitution, even though what is written into our fundamental law does suggest a moderate bias against such "injustice." I said a moderate bias, but no more than that. Therefore I am surprised to read in Charles Fairman's majestic *History of the Supreme Court of the United States: Reconstruction and Reunion, 1864–1888* that "the Thirteenth Amendment introduced a revolutionary change in the relation of the United States to the State governments."[26] My understanding of the evidence is much more conservative. As I see the matter, the authors of these amendments and laws confronted the question of whether or not they should suspend the Constitution every time they found a worthy cause that asked them to do so in order to achieve specific noble objectives. Already they had changed some of the circumstances in which various kinds of Americans might interact. However, what signifies is that, even without the presence of traditional Southern restraints on such legislative adventures, even with so many radicals present in their company, they refused to put a cause first and constitutional morality second, which is more than we can say for some of their interpreters.

If Hyman and Wiecek are correct, if the Thirteenth Amendment did indeed signify that "all Americans were equal before all laws" and that "emancipation required positive duties upon government to secure all free men's rights against any offenders, governmental or private, in any guise," then there should be some evidence supportive of their view in the 1866 civil rights law. And there is not,[27] for the legislation clearly draws its authority from the Thirteenth Amendment—from its enactment clause.[28] The Framers of this amendment, as I said above, intended for it to give the freedman the protections that he enjoyed in what had been the old Northwest Territory, and in the states derived from that jurisdiction—that is, if he could win initial admission to those communities. These advantages did not include the right to vote or immunity to social discrimination. They did not include desegregated schools, railroad cars, housing, hotels, and so forth. But they were, given the power of racial feeling in those societies, none the less noteworthy, in most cases marking improvements upon the predictable consequences of the old Black Codes of the Middle West: laws that had made it almost impossible for a black to migrate into Ohio, Indiana, or Illinois and support himself in those states with any security— unless he could get a white man to post a large bond to guarantee that he would be socially useful while living "free" (that is, perpetually in debt and therefore in a servile condition). Southern states after the forcible restoration of the Union had passed their own Black Codes that, in 1865, seemed to most Republicans to nullify emancipation. Hence arises a civil rights law that had as its benchmark what was, in 1865, allowed in Lincoln's Illinois—the midwestern state that almost always resisted every step in the direction of equal status for blacks.[29]

Northern Democrats, to be sure, warned that the bill might signify a great deal more—might disturb established social and legal patterns in the North. In 1867–74 they won major political battles by insisting on "the Constitution as it was." In answer to their scare tactics Congressman Rutherford B. Hayes in 1866 wrote, "I know it [the 1866 act] is grossly misrepresented and greatly misunderstood in Ohio. *The Commercial* [Cincinnati] speaks of it as if it gives increased and unheard of rights as privileges to negroes—as if it would compel the schools to receive negro children, the hotels negro guests, etc etc etc now please to note what I say. It undertakes to secure the negro no right which he has not enjoyed in Ohio since the repeal of the Black Laws in 1848–9." [30] These rights, as indicated by my short list above, were not many. And even that little was thought by some Republican congressmen, such as Ohio radical John A. Bingham, to be more than the Thirteenth Amendment could authorize since "the care of the property, the liberty, and the life of the citizen, under the . . . Federal Constitution, is in the States, and not in the Federal Government." [31] By reason of the currency of such opinions, when the Republicans thereafter readopted the 1866 civil rights law, they did so under the Fourteenth and Fifteenth amendments, not the Thirteenth. [32]

Now we may of course reason again from silence and maintain that the intentions of the authors of this amendment and the civil rights law attached to it were left unstated as a subterfuge so that the lawmakers might deceive one another and all the people who had sent them to Congress. Reasoning so, we might find in the absence of specification the implication that every right imaginable is guaranteed by such silence, and that the way to correct one evil was, in the opinion of these Americans, to commit another—to engage in duplicity in the making of the laws. Hyman and Wiecek speak of rights "not discoverable in any printed record, including congressional debates" and mutter in apology for the heroes of their narrative that they "knew how uncertain the legal literature was on rights," leaving therefore "blanks" for their posterity to fill in. This is a pleading *ad ignorantium.* We can be satisfied that Hyman and Wiecek have done their best as friendly expositors of what was said and done in "the best cause Americans had ever perceived." [33] But if we reason thus we may just as well pretend that black is white, up down, justice deception, and the law whatever we make up as we go along.

*T*he civil rights law of 1866, the Fourteenth Amendment (passed by Congress June 13, 1866), and the civil rights laws of 1870 and 1871 got the Republican Party into a great deal of political difficulty, as did the Fifteenth Amendment and, somewhat later, the civil rights law of 1875. After a high tide in 1866, in 1867 the Republicans lost in Ohio, Connecticut, and Pennsylvania. They gave ground in every state but Michigan and Kentucky. In Kansas, Minnesota, New Jersey, and Ohio proposals for extension of the suffrage to blacks failed. Later they failed again in Michigan and Pennsylvania. Colorado and Nebraska applied to be admitted to the Union without giving a franchise to blacks. And there was more and worse to come. Many congressmen were defeated—especially radical Republicans. Ben Wade was beaten in Ohio as were Republican governors in California and Connecticut. Furthermore, it was clear from the first that 1868 and 1870, 1872 and 1874 could bring more of the same, even though Grant ran ahead of the ticket and his party remained in power. But his triumph was not a victory for Charles Sumner and his friends. Neither was the Republican triumph of 1872.[34] The winners were a new breed of Republicans who saw power as an end in itself and the abolitionist tradition (as opposed to military success) as a doubtful inheritance. By fragile margins, Republican votes from the South prolonged the hegemony of the party for a while—electoral votes and Senate seats won by the bayonet, by graft, manipulation, and vote fraud. But in 1874 the Grand Old Party lost effective control of both houses. It left office while passing a curious, petulant civil rights bill that it expected to see repealed or overturned in the courts but hoped might result in a few black votes. Its policy on rights was by 1874 perceived as part of a large and dishonorable design to stay in power through pretended idealism, and as a liability among the rank and file of Northern voters. The public view of this Republican behavior was sound—regardless of the elaborate exercises of John Cox and LaWanda Cox.[35] But the momentum of this business was broken earlier, in 1867–68. Only by occupation and the disfranchisement of Southerners was it sustained for another seven years—in puppet regimes established and/or preserved by Yankee judges, bureaucracy, and garrisons.

It is an absolute consensus of the scholarship that there was, in states that had been loyal to the Union, no popular demand for all of this legislation.[36] Yet, it must be admitted, there were those in the Congress and without who wished each of the Reconstruction measures to mean a great deal more than they did. They were a minority—the radical Republicans, who are now sometimes identified as representative Americans of their time.

Much modern judicial ingenuity has been built upon a broad view, the radical Republican view, of the language concerning "due process of law" in section 1 of the Fourteenth Amendment. Earlier inventions depended upon the passage concerning "privileges and immunities" in the same section. Yet anything in this series of Reconstruction innovations in law can be (and has been) a basis for expanding the outreach of federal authority, especially (but not exclusively) in the matter of personal rights. Through its connection to that old workhorse, the 1866 civil rights law, even the Thirteenth Amendment can still function as a point of departure for judicial flights of fancy—as in *Jones v. Alfred H. Mayer Co.* (1968), *Sullivan v. Little Hunting Park* (1969), *Tillman v. Wheaton-Haven Recreational Association* (1973), *Johnson v. Railway Express Agency* (1975), *Runyon v. McCrary* (1976), and *McDonald v. Santa Fe Trail Transportation Co.* (1976). In particular *Jones v. Alfred H. Mayer Co.*, 392 U.S. 409 (1968), serves as an epitome of how little intellectual integrity may sometimes be found in even the most august and distinguished of American jurists and attorneys. The case turns on the particular details of history and argues toward a decision that supposedly conforms to an original intention invoked by the High Court. It is no exercise in "higher law" interpretation, structuralist ingenuity, or "critical" legal studies, but a traditional exposition of the law in the context in which it was made. It can therefore be judged on those grounds. And in that context the Supreme Court's decision was palpably ridiculous—a bit of posturing in the best tradition of abolitionist historiography.

To be sure there were certain personal rights specified under the 1866 civil rights law and the Fourteenth Amendment: the "privileges of citizens; the privilege of buying, selling and enjoying property; the privilege of engaging in any lawful employment for a livelihood; the privilege of resorting to the laws and the like."[37] These protections were more or less what the freedmen could expect in the Midwest in 1866–70. But they did not, for blacks, include the franchise, or securities against discrimination by private citizens, or a right to purchase from people who did not wish to sell, or access to integrated schools or graveyards, or the license to practice a profession, or the right to marry outside their race. Though in the case of this last restriction some Republicans argued there was no injustice in the prohibition because both races were equally restrained.[38]

In every case these changes did not alter the nomocratic character of the American regime because they did not predicate a particular result so much as a change of context. Moreover, the obvious evidence ignored in decisions such as the one handed down in *Jones v. Alfred H. Mayer Co.* is that all of these innovations are a sequence, must be read as a sequence, with what was added in the Fifteenth Amendment and the civil rights laws of 1870, 1871, and 1875 clearly not a part of what earlier laws provided in the way of personal rights. Finally, even those laws and that amendment did not reach after the kind of drastic change in the guaranteed rights of citizens which the radical Republicans felt that justice required. Furthermore, though they confronted the established values of an American society cautiously, without violating a federalism in conflict with an absolute commitment to enforced equality, they were recognized as falling short of their modest purposes even before these were approved by the Congress—as either (in the case of the laws) unconstitutional according to the Court's ruling in the Slaughter House Cases (1873) or (in the case of the amendment) unable to secure the promised result, even when ratified. For the laws and amendment did not intrude upon those corners of American life traditionally unregulated by law or touched only by local or state authorities because they were essentially negative in character, restraining certain conduct but not mandating a specific result.

In his monumental *Reconstruction and Reunion, 1864–88*, a contribution to the *Oliver Wendell Holmes Devise History of the Supreme Court of the United States*, Charles Fairman makes an example of the shoddy scholarship of the Warren Court in a detailed analysis of *Jones v. Alfred H. Mayer Co.* I must recapitulate his analysis in brief in order to turn its substance to the purposes of my argument here, to make it speak to the question of what the years that he surveys did to the formal nature of the Constitution as a nomocratic fundamental law. Justice Potter Stewart speaks for the Court in this case. He insists that the 1866 Congress had "a broad vision of the task before it." [39] He invokes the spirit of Senators Sumner and Wilson of Massachusetts and contemplates "sweeping effects." But chiefly he depends upon the idea of the law, *this law*, as a great lever of progressive change and not as protection for a known and established felicity. He maintains that the 1866 Civil Rights Act was constructed to do much more than repeal Black Codes in the South — laws that ostensibly undermined the emancipation — that the Act was drafted "to apply throughout the country" with "language . . . far broader than would have been necessary to strike down discriminatory statutes."[40] In this judgment he ignores the evidence recorded in the *Congressional Globe* that members of Congress spoke of little else in their 1866 debates but the necessity of correcting those recently adopted Southern statutes. Of Congressman John A. Bingham's opinion, agreed to by most of his colleagues, that only the special circumstances of Reconstruction, of recent emancipation and Southern efforts to establish peonage in the place of chattel slavery, can justify a limited intrusion into the domestic affairs of once rebellious states, Justice Stewart acknowledges nothing: or of other evidence (some of it examined above) of the limited list of rights covered by this first Reconstruction civil rights statute.[41] He therefore concludes that the 1866 law "bars all racial discrimination, private as well as public, in the sale or rental of property" — in absolute indifference to what was politically possible for the Thirty-ninth Congress to attempt and to all of the relevant legislative history, which he is eager to misrepresent.[42] Wherever possible, he quotes bits of speeches that appear to support his views and especially radical language contained in clauses rejected by Congress as a whole. He draws especial authority from a phrase removed from the bill because, in the language of its opponents, it "might give warrant for a latitudinarian construction not intended."[43] Anachronistically he assumes that midwestern senators were politically at liberty to authorize the Second Reconstruction that he strains with "desperate earnestness" to bring about in his own day. And he ignores what must be inferred from the absence of any provision for a civil penalty in the statute on which he depends — the implication that it was not expected to reach and regulate the actions of private persons.[44] Finally he falls back on the Thirteenth Amendment as authorizing the order of the Court and the power that it presupposes, leaving for the "majestic generalities" of the Fourteenth only a supporting role. Fairman concludes with the observation that those modern assumptions which evaluate a law in relation to the ends that it serves (a definition that cannot comprehend, in an issue touching rights, a small law and a narrow amendment to sanction it) have created a court with "no feeling for the truth of history."[45]

Yet in this case Stewart makes "a studied pronouncement on a matter of history," drafted in support of such abstract ends: the kind of pronouncement that has deflected previous studies of my subject. The Warren Court did not understand the relation of "finding the law" to consensus politics, the overwhelming approval necessary to validate drastic changes in the values of a society, the fact that judicial authority combined with casuistry cannot make legitimate what a nation's sense of itself rejects. And therefore cannot understand the difference between 1868 and 1968. "Majestic generalities" of the kind that have ruined the modern court are such as characterize a teleocratic fundamental law and appear to authorize judicial activism. Because of the constitutional morality of the mainline Republicans who put their oath to uphold the Constitution above politics or personal values, they are not to be found (these "generalities") in the Thirteenth Amendment (with enactment clause) or in the 1866 Civil Rights Act—measures "intended to counteract and furnish redress against state laws and proceedings" that really, as Justice Bradley maintained in the 1883 Civil Rights Cases, reached no further, contained no authority to pursue all the evil "incidents of slavery."[46] Or any other evils. And neither does the Fourteenth, which has become the most important of the Reconstruction measures here under consideration and the linchpin of the modern judicial revolution conducted in the name of assorted "rights."

When, *under very unusual and never properly adjudicated circumstances*, the Fourteenth Amendment was finally adopted on July 9, 1868, few Americans could have imagined how it might someday threaten to swallow up the rest of the United States Constitution. Most of the discussion in the Congress antecedent to the approval of this amendment concerned its Sections 2 and 3. Yet it is Section 1 that is, for us, *the* Fourteenth Amendment. The rest of the document is an uncomfortable reminder that it is designed to work toward the Reconstruction of a subjugated South. The Framers of this amendment (such as Senator John Sherman) thought it was "only an embodiment of the Civil Rights Bill."[47] Moreover, to repeat a central theme of this essay, it is part of a sequence of laws and amendments— which is to say that it begins in a tendentious political act, not in Olympian disinterestedness and spiritual triumph over racial animosity. This amendment had as its primary purpose a plan to do something for the Republican Party by controlling a rebellious South, which meant that it did incidentally a few things for blacks, whose help would be needed if Republicans were to stay in power. But not too much. And certainly not at the level of personal relations. In Section 1 appear what Senator Sherman of Ohio spoke of as "glittering generalities which I like to see from time to time": language forbidding action by the states to abridge the "privileges and immunities" of citizens of the United States; other language (echoing the Magna Carta) preventing the states (or persons using state law) from depriving citizens of "life, liberty or property" without "due process of law," guaranteeing all such citizens "equal protection of the laws."[48] Herewith things are changed a little, the balance of federalism altered with another negative, like the provision in the original Constitution providing for trial by jury in Article III, Section 2 and an equivalent provision in the Seventh Amendment. All of which is to protect *some* federal rights—rights of federal citizenship, also granted to the freedman (in answer to Dred Scott) in the same text—at the state level. And nothing new at all appears in the formal pattern of the Constitution—especially if we remember that the language concerning due process goes back to Lord Coke on the thirty-ninth chapter of the Great Charter, to 25 Edw. III st 5, c. 4 (1352), and 28 Edw. III, c. 3 (1354). This is no trifling "legislative history" for the restraint of judicial invention.[49] What it meant was merely that these things should be done in the usual way or not at all. It had to do with trial procedure, and with related matters, not with the acts of a legislator or a private person involved in those encounters among individuals not regulated at law. Language about "due process" appears in the Fifth Amendment to the 1787 Constitution and, before 1868, showed little potential for inflation from a negative into a positive—a notion of substantive due process, which amounts to the granting of authority over law to a set of antecedent "natural rights." No written constitution or limited government of laws such as the Framers intended can coexist with such a doctrine.

No one who has examined the detailed legislative history surrounding the adoption of the Fourteenth Amendment can have any doubt that the purpose of its Framers was to protect blacks from discrimination with respect to specified fundamental rights, enumerated in the Civil Rights Act and epitomized in the privileges and immunities clause. As Raoul Berger maintains, "enumeration," according to the Framers, marked the bounds of the grant.[50] There was "an all but universal understanding that the Amendment was to embody the Civil Rights Act."[51] In this embodiment (making revocations following some future Democratic victory difficult) and its prototype, *some* change was made in the balance of powers between state and national government—a change following from the fundamental innovation of emancipation. The grant of citizenship was a logical corollary of these small shifts in the pattern. The rest of the amendment was mere politics and postbellum revenge—attempts to reduce the future influence of the South on national affairs, to disfranchise the white population of that region, and to preclude burdensome litigation over Southern claims. Of course, the entire amendment is a context for discovering the meaning of its first section: a framework that warns us not to look for universal truth or Apollonian disinterestedness in the document. It is a piece of business made for its place and time, in the lofty language Republicans liked to use in rationalizing their objectives yet, at its heart, partisan. But it is more than tautology or vacuous reaffirmation of promises contained in the 1787 Constitution. In order to prevent mischief by construction, Justice Samuel Miller, speaking for the Chase Court, goes so far in his ruling in the Slaughter House Cases, 16 Wall. 36 [1873], as to abstract most of the Civil Rights Act of 1866 from the meaning of the first section of the Fourteenth Amendment—leaving protected only rights that "owe their existence to the Federal Government, its national character, its constitution or its law." Among these were rights specified in the original Constitution plus protection overseas, access to ports and navigable streams. Rights determined under state citizenship included everything else covered at law. He admits that "gross injustice" to freedmen as a matter of concern to the 1866 law, under the Fourteenth Amendment, would allow "suitable legislation" but only after-the-fact legislation.[52]

Miller was fearful that any other ruling might subject to "the Control of the Congress . . . the entire domain of civil rights belonging exclusively to the states," or that the Supreme Court might become "a perpetual censor upon all legislation of the States, on the civil rights of their own citizens."[53]

So great a departure from "the structure and spirit of our institutions," he believed, "must be rejected"; it would "fetter and degrade the State governments." [54] Justice Miller, in drafting his opinion, was working in a sensible direction, toward a balanced view of our national bond as modified by the Reconstruction amendments. His interpretation was one that did not see in these enactments "any purpose to destroy the main features of the general system." But, given the nature of our Constitution, with the space provided in its form for the addition of discrete, particular powers without compromise to the basic division and limitations of and on the authorities that it creates, it was not necessary for him to cancel Section 1 of the Fourteenth Amendment. In this matter the position taken by Justice Stephen Field that this amendment "was adopted to obviate objections which had been raised and pressed with great force to the validity of the Civil Rights Act" is sufficient. As part of the Constitution, this protection for the freedman would be secure. Berger accurately observes that "in holding that the Amendment was designed to assure . . . equality with respect to certain specified rights among residents of a state, Justice Field staked out a position . . . that honestly reflected the intention of the Framers." [55] The amendment did not provide authority over "all legislation" but dealt with state and local laws that worked against specific rights: rights indicated by "the first section of the Civil Rights Act." Yet unfortunately he argued to this conclusion from an expansive view of the privileges and immunities clause, suggesting its outreach in fostering equality "among citizens of the United States" — in their capacities as citizens of the Republic — by making reference to the Declaration, to the vapidities of Justice Bushrod Washington in *Corfield v. Coryell*, 6 Fed. Cases 546, No. 3230 (C.C.E.D. Pa. 1823), and to inalienable "rights which are the gift of the Creator; which the law does not confer but only recognizes." [56] It is Justice Miller's opinion that keeps absolutely clear of any language having to do with the generic equality of humankind, and of metaphysical, prepolitical natural rights — as do the Thirteenth Amendment, the Civil Rights Act of 1866, and the Fourteenth Amendment. In this Miller follows the law rather than making it. Within a few years the High Court began to combine the best elements from the opinions of Miller and Field in dealing with this part of the Constitution and to find a thread of consistency in all that Congress had said and done in promoting Reconstruction.

Our understanding of the Fourteenth Amendment, and especially of its first section, is beclouded by the greatest variety and volume of interpretive distortion attached to any component of the United States Constitution. What I refer to is a paragraph smothered over the generations by the concoctions of those advanced spirits always more interested in speaking of what it should have meant, or might become, or of the "general principles" concealed beneath it than they are in what the law, interpreted through what the Republican majority in the Congress in April, May, and June 1866 might have been politically free to undertake, means on its face. There is no way for legitimate commentary on this text to avoid the plethora of evidence from legislative history preserved in the *Congressional Globe* and *Record*—especially when this material is illuminated by certain contemporary press accounts and by the papers of important participants in the history of the times. Concerning the intentions embodied in the drafting of the Fourteenth Amendment, this record is so homogeneous as to require at this point no more than a summary and sampling of its volume and near unanimity. In debates recorded in the *Globe* for May 8 and 9, 1866, Benjamin M. Boyer of Pennsylvania, Martin Russell Thayer of Pennsylvania, James A. Garfield of Ohio, Henry Raymond of New York, and other members put beyond doubt the purpose of the Republican majority in passing the first section of the Fourteenth Amendment.[57] They say what their purpose is, which no cunning or distortion can evade. Elsewhere, even the patron saint of the Republican radicals, Thaddeus Stevens of Pennsylvania, indicates his agreement with them—that these measures "do not touch social or political rights."[58] And there is other speech to the same effect recorded from what Republican senators said in their debates on the amendment.[59] Charles Sumner of Massachusetts, finding so little in the way of revolutionary transformation of the Constitution authorized in the Fourteenth Amendment, gave it almost no support.[60] And others of his ilk actively opposed it—including such fiery spirits as Wendell Phillips.

But it is not this consensus of opinions, explicated according to the canons of rhetoric and the ordinary methods of literary analysis, that attracts the attention of those who wish to make the most of the amendment. Instead, they focus on the opinions of one congressman, John A. Bingham of Ohio, and especially on a speech that he made five years after the fact of his role in passing the amendment; and on another address by Senator Jacob Howard of Michigan, who was, without time for proper preparation, obliged to present the amendment to the Upper House when Senator Fessenden of Maine fell ill. Neither Bingham nor Howard was in any way a barometer of political sentiment in their respective chambers. In addition, Bingham was often inconsistent, contradictory, and ignorant of the business of Congress; and Howard, during the drafting of the Fourteenth Amendment, was unprepared, foolish, and unrepresentative of its authors when pretending to represent them.[61] But those who broadly interpret the Fourteenth Amendment do even worse than depend upon the meandering vapidities of Bingham and the self-righteous carelessness of Howard. For their most outrageous strategy is in using exaggerated Democratic objections to the first section of the amendment—objections that attribute to it a centralizing power which few Republicans wished it to include, instances of what rhetoricians call the *diaboli*. In the process they forced Congressional advocates of this language to narrow its meaning further and further, by gloss and commentary, as debate on the amendment and its ratification ran its course.[62] Ultimately they found their defense, a protection against the worst charges of the Democrats, in the language of the Civil Rights Act itself: "[that] inhabitants of every race shall have the same right to make and enforce contracts, to sue, be parties and give evidence, to inherit, purchase, lease, sell, hold and convey real and personal property, and to full and equal benefit of all laws and proceedings for the security of person and property."[63] But in this language there is absolutely no comfort for the broad view of the Fourteenth Amendment. Therefore those who presently interpret it "for our time" have given up on history, fallen back on obfuscatory generalizations about how little can be known, and have insisted that it is best for us not to worry about such matters so long as we follow the "hallowed principles" that undergird the Constitution and determine (once we have "deconstructed" it by our exegesis) its present meaning, however it came into our hands. These arguments release from scholarly restraint the random genius of interpretation that has found as many ways of reading the first section of the Fourteenth Amendment as literary critics have employed to explain Milton's mysterious image of the "two-handed engine" in "Lycidas." And to as little purpose!

Usually, however, these farfetched readings come down to one proposition: that the amendment "contains language capable of growth"; that "those who drafted Section 1 [of the Fourteenth Amendment] intended that the meanings of these phrases should evolve and expand with the passage of time and changes of circumstance." [64] Or, to rephrase the doctrine with specific reference to the United States Supreme Court, Section 1 "has a role as expounder of basic national ideals of individual liberty and fair treatment, even when the content of those ideals is not expressed as a matter of positive law in the Constitution." [65] From these assumptions it is not difficult to reach the conclusion that "whatever the Framers of the Fourteenth intended, there is no reason to believe that they possessed the best insights or ultimate wisdom as to the meaning of their words for subsequent generations," or to reach any other conclusion that can better be described as augury of the future soon to unfold than as the truth about the Constitution.[66] Of course, in the end we get Chief Justice Warren saying that "the provisions of the Constitution are not time worn adages or hollow shibboleths . . . . [but] vital living principles." And also get Warren's academic apologists coming after him, arguing that the Court had always from the Founders the "implied power" to revise and rewrite the Constitution according to its recognition of a "higher" or "natural law." [67] Taken together, their words describe according to its essence just what a teleocratic constitution might be, or describe no constitution at all.

*F*or the story of the Fifteenth Amendment, which became law on March 30, 1870, we can return to *The Right to Vote: Politics and the Passage of the Fifteenth Amendment* and *Retreat from Reconstruction, 1869–1879* by William Gillette [68] and to *North of Reconstruction: Ohio Politics, 1869–1870* by Felice A. Bonadio.[69] The beginning of all commentary on this amendment is that, since it provides that the freedman shall not be denied the vote by reason of his color, we can reasonably determine that the Thirteenth and Fourteenth amendments and the Civil Rights Act of 1866 did not reach that far. The voting amendment is once again a discrete and particular measure in its objectives and in the authority that it creates. From language that was explicitly rejected by its Framers, we may with confidence conclude that it was not drawn "to offset state power to impose" voter qualifications. Moreover, it claimed no authority over private acts not performed under color of law.[70] Its authors had opportunities to make this amendment much more ambitious. They chose not to do so. Their plan was much smaller. What they hoped for was primarily to enlarge the black vote in the North, where blacks might make the difference in as many as seven states. Republicans in the Congress were urged to support this amendment as a "party" measure, a concession to partisan necessity, but not on its own merits or "for the sake of" blacks. And as a way of preventing the return to power of these old enemies of the Republic, the Southerners and Democrats—a way of remaining in power—it was also sold in the states. Discussion of the politics of this amendment is almost the only kind of discussion that is preserved from those who put it in place. They spoke of little else. For no other argument could have secured its passage.[71] Yet after adoption of the amendment many Republicans who represented communities hostile to the idea of blacks voting congratulated themselves on the resolution of the nation's long ordeal in completing the work begun with the war. They were also pleased at having effected this metamorphosis without injuring the Constitution—without taking away from the states their capacity to restrict the franchise or giving to the general government the responsibility to redefine Federalism in order to produce an electorate containing specific components. In other words, black voting could be discouraged anywhere according to this amendment—that is, for any reason other than race, according to any other measure, test, or formula. All of this origin, context, and modification marks the Fifteenth Amendment as no teleocratic innovation.

Yet even within a short time, and in the North as well as in the South, the amendment cost the Republicans votes and was, in the states that were being (or had been) reconstructed, resisted with energy. In many cases, blacks were prevented from reelecting generally despised, exploitive, venal, and irresponsible Republican state governments and officeholders. These had been imposed on a defeated South soon after Appomattox but could no longer be propped up by force alone. Southern Republicans, fearing the emergence of a politically "solid South," called for assistance from their friends in Congress and were not ignored. Men such as Senator Lyman Trumbull of Illinois spoke of legislation to be offered "for political purposes."[72] He spoke thus of measures like the Enforcement Act of May 31, 1870, dealing with official state action, and the Enforcement Act of February 28, 1871, setting up machinery to ensure fairness in federal elections. I have earlier called these the civil rights laws of 1870 and 1871. They were reinforced by other laws aimed at countering the activities of the Ku Klux Klan and at expanding enforcement powers outlined in the earlier laws. The target of much of this legislation was not, however, Southern misconduct but Democrats and their growing strength in the cities of the North—in particular by voting blacks in numbers that would cancel the influence of recent immigrants and the disaffected "Mugwump" Republicans in close elections. In the 1876 decision in *United States v. Cruikshank*, 92 U.S. 542, and subsequent decisions the Court narrowed the meaning of the Fifteenth Amendment. Many Republicans were actually relieved by this ruling, after being disenchanted by the political results of black voting and worried that they might, in the name of "human rights," do something that would seriously injure the balance of federalism in the Constitution. The nation's patience with the seemingly endless labor of "trampling out the grapes of wrath" was almost exhausted. So the Fifteenth Amendment had only a marginal effect on the national government's responsibility under the Constitution. And the laws attached to it, which might have made a difference, were nullified by the Court.

But in 1873–74 the Republicans tried once more, bringing forward (again in an effort to impress the same Northern black voters) the most radical of all of their reform measures, fulfilling, after his death, the wildest dreams of Charles Sumner and his friends. The Civil Rights Act of 1866, called by one of its best interpreters an "insignificant victory," had been undercut by the Court's ruling in the 1873 Slaughter House Cases even before it was brought to a vote by a lame-duck session of the Forty-third Congress. As Bernard Schwartz observes, enough of the supporters of this broad antidiscrimination law expressed doubts about its constitutionality to demonstrate that there was never a serious majority gathered behind it.[73] Moreover, as many as ninety of its supporters had lost their seats in the House of Representatives before they could be brought to vote for it—had been ruined by the rumor of their willingness to go beyond civil and political rights, even though they did not include in their legislation housing or schools, employment or racially inclusive graveyards. The Civil Rights Act of 1875 had been a "bomb" that "blew apart," causing a "counterrevolution in the North" even before the Congress voted to adopt it.[74] And after being included in the law, it became an immediate dead letter, with no one much interested in enforcing it and a legion of federal judges waiting to strike it down. In 1883 Justice Joseph Bradley ruled that Sections 1 and 2 of the 1875 law were not authorized by provisions of the Thirteenth and Fourteenth amendments. Moreover, even state and local governments were restrained from being discriminatory only in certain specific connections—such as had been identified by earlier decisions that had narrowed the meaning of other Reconstruction amendments and laws. At this point, after this ruling by Justice Bradley, there was no basis in the Constitution as modified since 1865 for interference with private acts of social, economic, or cultural preference. Add to *United States v. Cruikshank* and the Civil Rights Cases such decisions as *Strauder v. West Virginia*, 100 U.S. 303 (1880), *Ex parte* Virginia, 100 U.S. 339 (1880), *Hodges v. United States*, 203 U.S. 1 (1906), *Plessy v. Ferguson*, 163 U.S. 537 (1896), and *Corrigan v. Buckley*, 271 U.S. 323 (1926), and the reading of this 1865–75 portion of our nation's legal history here advanced is identified with what was the consensus of the High Court's opinion on such questions for fifty years after the last of these measures won the approval of the Congress. For those who have read the legislative history behind these amendments and laws and who know the political history (and, to be fair, the constitutional rectitude) that produced them, it is apparent that their official interpretations could not have been meaningfully different from what they were in 1883. No court interested primarily in reading the law could have made a better finding. It requires another approach to constitutional interpretation to construe the available evidence another way—and a teleocratic view of the purpose of our fundamental law. During the years of their domination of the nation's political life, the Republicans who had fought and won the War Between the States were (probably because of their devotion to liberty) unwilling to make that teleocratic view their own.

*W*hat then is the burden of the constitutional history* that I have here summarized all too briefly in its relation to a particular view of the original Constitution of the United States as one kind of fundamental law? First of all, this record, contrary to the observation of Leonard Levy in his

"Introduction" to *The Fourteenth Amendment and the Bill of Rights: The Incorporation Theory* by Charles Fairman and Stanley Morrison, proves that for the expositor of the Constitution the "greater issue" is not "Should the Bill of Rights be incorporated into the total Constitution?" but "Is it thus incorporated through the agency of the Fourteenth Amendment?" [75] Justice is the business of the lawgiver, acting through the process that gives him agency under the Constitution. This division of labors means, in the case of fundamental changes, amendments. Or in the case of lesser changes, it leads to application of standing provisions of the Constitution through positive laws—statutes that rest on a more tenuous footing than amendments because they require only a majority vote, and that can be undone as easily as they are made: repealed or disallowed by the courts when found to be in violation of the terms of the national bond of union.

In the end, in handing on to our posterity "a government of laws and not of men," in sustaining the authority of the fundamental law by preserving the process by which it is properly made, protecting its legitimacy as reflective of the nation's deliberate and well-established sense of itself, its "implicit principle," we accomplish something far more important than any guarantee of the ability of all citizens to buy a sandwich wherever food is prepared; or to have equal influence over the selection of the next commissioner's court; or the right to be equally represented by group in the student body of any public school. Legitimate change in the Constitution can be made only by amendment—not by the will of the High Court, its well-meaning, teleocratic misuse of its originally narrow and specific role within the law. For if it does not keep the law, who will? And if the law itself is personalized or politicized at its source, who among us is secure?

Today there is obviously a more than antiquarian reason for examining the Reconstruction amendments and laws as they have been understood at various times since their adoption: for remembering how little (apart from questions of commercial regulation) they meant to the Waite Court and the Fuller Court—and even to White and Taft. The modern rejection of the Court's 1875–1925 position on personal rights and equal protection has been the cutting edge in the transformation of the United States Constitution into an ostensibly teleocratic fundamental law. These readings have become the models for other distortions dealing with things beyond the freedman and his descendants. It is therefore an interpretation that must be discredited before it leads to more and more serious abuses of the text. From all of this exfoliation of imaginary rights we learn several lessons: that constitutional morality requires our assent to the doctrine that there is no revision of the Constitution but by amendment; that Lincoln and Taney and all the Founders are correct in insisting that "the intent of the lawgiver is the law"; that we can bear no imposition by judges upon the people of what the Court sometimes calls "enlightened opinion"; that we must be content to find in the Constitution at any point in our history only the authority to correct those conditions covered by its jurisdiction, resisting the temptation to push it beyond its nature because of our enthusiasm for some worthy purpose or cause.

Finally, we must remember to ask of our countrymen that they expect no more of government than Pierce Butler of South Carolina described in the Great Convention as "the best they would receive." For the reform of the regime by construction is (to quote Butler once more—in this instance following Plutarch) an "innovation" that "the people will not bear," or rather will not tolerate and still remain free.[76] To condense much history, it is the truth recognized by the High Court in the years following the Slaughter House Cases decision of 1873. If we wish to see substantive changes in the bond, let us persuade two-thirds of the Congress and three-fourths of the states to agree. If they refuse, we must wait upon them to change their minds: wait and submit to the wisdom of the Framers in making the amending process very difficult indeed. For by this means may we effect reforms and still honor our oath to preserve, protect, and defend the Constitution.

According to the teleocratic view of fundamental law that conceives of it as chiefly instrumental, there is no such thing as constitutional morality. Moreover, where illegitimate construction has planted within that fundamental law excrescences that continue to poison the body politic, even conservatives are reluctant to recognize that the corruption must be removed, whatever the cost in temporary disruption—surgically removed, lest the infection get forever beyond control. I admit that those who have an investment in constitutional distortion will cry out in a rage for abstract justice once such a drastic amputation has occurred. But in the long run all Americans would profit from the restoration of constitutional integrity, and from the recovery of another kind of justice, one in keeping with who and what we are as a people—the nomocratic continuity of our first two hundred years.

EPILOGUE

The Comforting Delusion

If I have learned one thing from reading in the constitutional history of the United States and from traveling as a speaker on that subject throughout the Republic during the years of our bicentennial celebration, it is that the old confusion between the Constitution and the language concerning equality in the Declaration of Independence persists, even now, almost unabated. Indeed, I might well argue that it grows to be more and more entrenched with each passing decade. The delusion that is sustained by this conflation is a modern version of the ancient *argumentum ad populum*. Or at least our politicians have often thought that it was—as do many of the clergy, teachers, journalists, and other makers of public opinion—for they do not know the Constitution or how we came to have it. Whenever I gave these addresses such progressive, sanguine souls were inclined to make objection to my analysis, speaking always out of the myth already in place even before adoption of the Reconstruction amendments. To the evidence that our Constitution is mostly procedural, with a few restraints on government attached in the Bill of Rights, they were oblivious; or, out of a doctrinaire spirit, obscurantist and ineducable. This delusion concerning the Framers of the Constitution is, to a certain conventional audience, comforting, and to Jacobin ideologues of the contemporary variety a sanction and encouragement. But it does not reflect a "law of the land" in any imaginable interpretation of that phrase or conform to any of the evidence examined in preceding chapters.

Of course, the United States Constitution is designed to promote justice under law. And to secure "to ourselves and our posterity the blessings of liberty" — though the "we" speaking thus are not a collectivity but are only citizens of at least one of the nine disparate majorities functioning severally in nine or more states. Moreover, even the most federal view of the new Union would allow that it followed the principle of self-government. But to "secure" liberties is to protect known and preexistent, historic rights, not all the same for every state or segment of the population. The concept invoked by that term does not imply the creation of something not yet in being.

To attempt to abstract from the Preamble to the Constitution a lever for transforming it into an instrumental document is, as Justice Story insisted in 1833, to live without (that is, outside) the law, to invent powers that do not exist.[1] And is also a transparent attempt to import the second paragraph of the Declaration — as a mandate for national self-re-creation, refounding — into our fundamental law. Yet no such action is required by the Preamble. No power is created by it. Rather, it explains what is intended by the rest of the document. A contemporary point of reference for all such nonsense as follows from an activist view of the Preamble and Declaration is Mortimer Adler's *We Hold These Truths*, a book "about" the Constitution whose weaknesses are specified by its very title.[2] After Adler identifies the Declaration as a "preface" to the Constitution, we know how his argument will tend: that in the end that Declaration will, if allowed, swallow up the Constitution — except for the Preamble, as ideologically construed.[3]

Adler's Constitution is, to be sure, a "growing" authority; and, as he concedes, it is very different from what the Framers had made. But he can find reasons for disagreeing with my view about that bright original: reasons for rejecting "a strict interpretation of the Constitution" as now recommended by interpretivist jurisprudence. Without recourse to unstated "ideals" visible only in the Preamble or Declaration, important (and widely accepted) "revisions" of the Constitution might never have occurred. Furthermore, in Adler's opinion, even more changes will be necessary. A future emphasis on inalienable economic rights will be required if political rights already achieved through legislation, judicial opinion, and a few "good" amendments are to produce finally "the realization of the democratic ideal that has recently become an objective of our Constitution."[4] The constitutional office of a Tribune of the People and that of Public Prosecutor, together with other like-minded innovations, are suggested — elements from an old, discredited list. But if these objectives for improving our fundamental law were not surprising enough, the way in which Adler manages to introduce them into a discussion is even more astonishing. The text of the Constitution proper plays no major role in the process, what Kurland properly identifies as its procedural surface, its emphasis on how the business of the nation is to be conducted.[5] Instead Adler speaks of the Declaration ("the architectural blueprint for the government of the United States"), the Preamble, and (because of its value as a *gloss* on the Declaration) the Gettysburg Address — "something *like* the sacred scriptures of this nation."[6]

Adler is a marvel of obdurate misconception and wishful thinking in *We Hold These Truths*, going so far in one place as to maintain that "almost all the underlying ideas of the Constitution are to be found in the second paragraph of the Declaration of Independence, in some phrases in Lincoln's Gettysburg Address and [only] here and there in the Constitution itself."[7] These ideas, he says, are "equality, inalienable rights (or human rights), the pursuit of happiness, civil rights (to secure human rights), the consent of the governed, and the dissent of the governed."[8] Adler's analysis would seem so weak as to embarrass his admirers — did it not concern equality. No critical thought on that subject is now encouraged. Indeed, it may soon be forbidden. The distance between Declaration and Constitution is given definitive exposition by the late Willmoore Kendall in his "Equality: Commitment or Ideal?" and was treated more recently by Jack N. Rakove.[9] The question concerning such distance was closed long ago. Yet Adler even claims that "the Declaration calls for the establishment of constitutional government" — when the truth is that this statement of many sovereign states acting collectively specifies that Americans lived already under a variety of constitutional governments, and had done so for some time when they sought their independence.

But my perception of the Aspen Institute's genial polymath and his conflation of law and philosophy does not so much attach to any of his writings as to a master class on the subject of *We Hold These Truths*, which in 1987 he taught on PBS to a group of students from St. John's College in Annapolis, Maryland. After a full presentation of Adler's theories, these young people would not agree with his merging of "is" with "ought" or with his inflated conception of the standing of natural rights in the Constitution. Adler responded that only the Constitution as it had emerged in response to its "underlying structure of principle" deserved the full tribute of bicentennial celebration: today's Constitution as an embodiment of abstract propositions. Or rather, the Constitution as it will some day exist — once it has completed this process of development in realizing principles. To the contrary, what the St. John's students reaffirmed was "the old teaching of the Fathers": that Americans do not wish to be governed by an omnicompetent, divinized state, so full of good intentions that it will stop at nothing to realize them. In a word, they did not wish to live such politicized lives; nor had their parents before them. But the necessity of resisting those who agree with Adler (from the beginning, they have been a problem) had, the St. John's students recognized, imposed on them — on the rest of us who prefer a nomocratic order (once more, see Oakeshott) — the obligations of partisan engagement.

In discussing the first ratification convention in North Carolina, I emphasized the reaction of James Iredell, William Richardson Davie, and most of their colleagues to a proposal that their convention draw up a statement on natural human rights in order to measure in specific the evidence of such doctrine in the proposed United States Constitution. From time to time, the same notion has carried over into deliberations on proposed amendments to the Constitution. And it was the subject of direct commentary in the opinion of Justice Iredell in *Calder v. Bull*, U.S. (3 Dallas) 186 (1793), where that subtle Burkean warned his colleagues on the High Court not to "disallow positive law" on "principles of natural justice" since "such ideas are regulated by no fixed standard" and are the causes of disagreement among "the ablest and purest of men." Iredell's friend General Davie had reasoned to the same effect at Hillsborough: reasoned against attempts to make a Constitution on the ground of theories concerning "unalienable rights," theories that went "against the nature of things." [10]

Contrary to what the enemies of Iredell and Davie maintained, contrary to Adler's customary argument, the American attitude toward claims that equality in the Declaration is the central text in American politics has generally been that the second paragraph of that document has not obliged us to follow a particular policy or enact a specific measure. In practice we have always recognized that in 1776 the states had authorized only a declaration of independence and not precisely the language of the Declaration they got. They were by vote committed only to that part of the Declaration that said they were free. Talk of the deferred promise of the Declaration went against the primary motives of the Framers: to revise the Articles and raise a revenue while preserving a limited government, one that honored their preference for a form of liberty which did not threaten prospects for voluntary unity or the hope of that virtue which grows only in a cultivated, "social" soil.

In a regime of independent freeholders, commercial men, and self-governing communities (who had negotiated informally their own version of a civil compact, one they could in good heart defend "together" without rewriting their common past and without any hope of reforming one another), such a balance was possible: a *federal* balance as that term signified to them. So they reassured one another with tiresome iteration. Concerning the Framers, these essays have, with the same kind of emphasis, demonstrated that, despite their many other differences, limited government (as opposed to anarchic freedom) was uniformly their objective. The evidence to that effect we should take seriously, even when we are personally inclined to think another way, for the alternative is dishonesty and contempt for the law.

NOTES

1. Such a Government as the People Will Approve

1. See Charles Warren, *The Making of the Constitution* (New York: Barnes and Noble, 1967), p. 140; also Walter Berns, *The Writing of the American Constitution* (Washington, D.C.: President's Commission on White House Fellowships, 1984), p. 14.

2. John P. Roche, "The Founding Fathers: A Reform Caucus in Action," *The Reinterpretation of the American Revolution, 1763–1789*, ed. Jack P. Greene (New York: Harper and Row, 1968), p. 445.

3. James Madison, *Notes of Debates in the Federal Convention of 1787* (Athens: Ohio University Press, 1966), p. 189.

4. Madison, *Notes*, p. 223.

5. These moderate men were not all agreed on what the Constitution should be, but were, disagreements aside, determined not to forfeit the opportunity before them because they had such an absolute devotion to their favorite ideas on the subject. Their spirit is that of Benjamin Franklin when, at the end of the convention (Madison, *Notes*, p. 654), he urges each of his colleagues to "doubt a little his own infallibility." See Forrest McDonald, *Novus Ordo Seclorum: The Intellectual Origins of the Constitution* (Lawrence: University Press of Kansas, 1985), p. 260.

6. Drawn from Aristotle, *Poetics*, trans. S. H. Butcher (New York: Hill and Wang, 1961), pp. 56 and 52.

7. Northrop Frye, *Fables of Identity: Studies in Poetic Mythology* (New York: Harcourt, Brace and World, 1963), p. 25.

8. Northrop Frye, *Anatomy of Criticism* (Princeton: Princeton University Press, 1957), p. 171.

9. Warren, *The Making of the Constitution*, p. 273; also Charles J. Stillé, *The Life*

and Times of John Dickinson, 1732–1808 (New York: Burt Franklin, 1969), p. 262; Madison, *Notes*, p. 118.

10. Madison, *Notes*, p. 239.

11. Ibid., p. 239.

12. Ibid., p. 31. Madison proposed such unacceptable laws because he was disgusted with what he had seen in the Continental Congress and the Virginia legislature. That he expected so much to be approved raises a question about his political judgment.

13. Madison, *Notes*, p. 44.

14. See *The Debates in the Several State Conventions on the Adoption of the Federal Constitution as Recommended by the General Convention at Philadelphia in 1787*, ed. Jonathan Elliot, 5 vols. (New York: J. B. Lippincott, 1876), 3:620.

15. Madison, *Notes*, p. 221.

16. Ibid., pp. 293, 232, 236, 243, 278, and 210.

17. Ibid., p. 271.

18. Ibid., p. 542.

19. Ibid., pp. 304–5.

20. Ibid., p. 156.

21. Ibid., p. 303.

22. Ibid., p. 89.

23. Ibid., p. 518.

24. Ibid., pp. 304, 159, and 87.

25. Ibid., pp. 305, 92, and 89.

26. Ibid., p. 74.

27. For a recent discussion of Madison's role in the Great Convention, see McDonald, *Novus Ordo Seclorum*, pp. 205–9. Also valuable is Lance Banning, "The Hamiltonian Madison: A Reconsideration," *Virginia Magazine of History and Biography* 92 (1984): 3–28. It is of course true that Madison briefly regressed toward his original centralizing disposition in attempting to make portions of the Bill of Rights apply to the states, and by advocating the inclusion in that supplement to the Constitution a broad theoretical declaration of rights. Here again wise men restrained him. See Elliot, *Debates*, 3:259 and 620–22, for samples of Madison, the mild Federalist.

28. The lines from Solon came to them by way of Montesquieu, *The Spirit of the Laws*, book 19, section 22. See Madison, *Notes*, pp. 73 and 229.

29. See Philip B. Kurland, "The Constitutional Impact of Public Policy: From the Warren Court to the Burger Court and Beyond," *World and I* 1, no. 8 (August

1986): 583: "A reading of the basic document will confirm my position that almost all of the Constitution is procedural, and not substantive in nature. It makes provision for how and by whom and in what areas public policy may be made rather than provision for what the substantive rules of governance are to be. Of course there are exceptions to this generalization. . . ." But generally, the substantive policy is left to be made by a branch of government authorized to do so by the Constitution. Kurland adds (p. 583) that Supreme Court Reports "are full to bursting with substantive constitutional commands. But for the most part, these are inventions or concoctions of the Supreme Court rather than commands of the Constitution."

John P. Diggins in his recent *The Lost Soul of American Politics: Virtue, Self-Interest, and the Foundations of Liberalism* (New York: Basic Books, 1984), pp. 48–68, explores the distance between the Declaration of Independence and the Constitution and concludes more or less as Kurland does: that the Constitution is not instrumental in its relation to any theory of natural rights.

30. McDonald, *Novus Ordo Seclorum*, p. 67.

31. Richard E. Welch, Jr., *Theodore Sedgwick, Federalist: A Political Portrait* (Middletown, Conn.: Wesleyan University Press, 1965), p. 60.

32. See Ralph Ketchum, *James Madison: A Biography* (New York: Macmillan, 1971), pp. 190–92. The struggle ran from 14 May 1787 throughout adjournment in September.

33. Elliot, *Debates*, 3:140–41.

34. See *The Writings of James Madison*, ed. C. Hunt, vol. 9 (New York: Putnam, 1910), p. 191.

2. The Best Constitution in Existence

1. Sir Henry Sumner Maine, *Popular Government* (London: John Murray, 1886), p. 253.

2. C. Ellis Stevens, *Sources of the Constitution of the United States, Considered in Relation to Colonial and English History* (New York: Macmillan, 1894), p. xi. Stevens also argues that "it is beginning to be realized [contra the enthusiasts of an American radical democracy, the local disciples of Rousseau] that the Constitution of the United States, though possessing elements of novelty, is not, after all, what this [radical idea of an invention *ex nihilo*] would imply. It is not, properly speaking, the original composition of one body of men, nor the outcome of one definite epoch, . . . it is better than that. It does not stand in historical isolation, free of

antecedents. It rests upon very old principles worked out by long ages of constitutional struggle. It looks back to the annals of the colonies and of the motherland for its sources and explanation" (pp. vi–viii).

3. Sir Herbert Butterfield, *The Englishman and His History* (Camden, Conn.: Archon Books, 1970), pp. 128–29.

4. Michael Kammen, *A Machine That Would Go of Itself: The Constitution in American Culture* (New York: Alfred A. Knopf, 1986), pp. 35–37, 156–84, 397–98.

5. For a summary of these British influences on our fundamental law, see Margaret A. Banks, "Drafting the American Constitution: Attitudes in the Philadelphia Convention Towards the British System of Government," *American Journal of Legal History* 10, no. 1 (1966): 15–33. For a partial documentation of this inheritance, one may examine the appropriate passages in *The Founders' Constitution*, ed. Philip B. Kurland and Ralph Lerner, 5 vols. (Chicago: University of Chicago Press, 1987).

6. Butterfield, *The Englishman and His History*, p. 58, from Lord Coke's sixth edition (London: n.p., 1681), pp. 45–47.

7. Quoted in Max Radin, "The Myth of Magna Carta," *Harvard Law Review* 60, no. 7 (1947): 1060. Radin notes that chapters 39 and 40 were combined into chapter 29 in the official Charter of Henry III (1224–25).

8. On Burke and the "Debates on the Canada Act," see the *Times*, 7 May 1791. Also see Carl B. Cone, *Burke and the Nature of Politics: The Age of the French Revolution* (Lexington: University Press of Kentucky, 1964), p. 81.

9. David S. Lovejoy, *The Glorious Revolution in America* (Middletown, Conn.: Wesleyan University Press, 1972); see also Lovejoy's "Two American Revolutions, 1689 and 1776," in *Three British Revolutions: 1641, 1688, 1776*, ed. J. G. A. Pocock (Princeton: Princeton University Press, 1980), pp. 244–62. The great merit of the Pocock book (and especially of the Robert Ashton essay "Tradition and Innovation and the Great Rebellion," which it includes [pp. 208–23]), is the way in which it brings home to us the retrospective continuity of Anglo-American legal history, reaching back so far as the time of Edward the Confessor.

10. Doris M. Stenton, *After Runnymede: Magna Carta in the Middle Ages* (Charlottesville: University Press of Virginia, 1964), p. 40.

11. See *The Debates in the Several State Conventions on the Adoption of the Federal Constitution as Recommended by the General Convention at Philadelphia in 1787*, ed. Jonathan Elliot, 5 vols. (New York: J. B. Lippincott, 1876), 3:170.

12. See *Letters of Delegates to Congress, 1774–1789*, ed. Paul H. Smith (Washington, D.C.: Library of Congress, 1976), 1:52–53 (debate of 8 September 1774).

13. Quoted in Kurland and Lerner, *Founders' Constitution*, 1:671.

14. Quoted in Frank Monaghan, *John Jay: Defender of Liberty* (New York: Bobbs-Merrill, 1935), p. 58.

15. George Dangerfield, *Chancellor Robert R. Livingston of New York, 1746–1813* (New York: Harcourt Brace, 1960), p. 82.

16. For language concerning "reconciliation . . . on constitutional principles," see *John Jay: The Making of a Revolutionary: Unpublished Papers, 1745–1780*, ed. Richard Morris (New York: Harper and Row, 1975), p. 200.

17. John Drayton, *Memoirs of the American Revolution, from Its Commencement to the Year 1776*, 2 vols. (Charleston: A. E. Miller, 1821), 1:260–61. I have commented previously on the constitutionalism of William Henry Drayton in *A Better Guide Than Reason: Studies in the American Revolution* (La Salle, Ill.: Sherwood Sugden and Co., 1979), pp. 111–33.

18. See David John Mays, *Edmund Pendleton, 1721–1803*, 2 vols. (Cambridge: Harvard University Press, 1952), 1:357.

19. See Griffith J. McCree, *The Life and Correspondence of James Iredell*, 2 vols. (New York: D. Appleton and Co., 1859), 1:136.

20. Letters for 11 February 1784 and 23 February 1786, preserved in State Archives, Raleigh, North Carolina.

21. Willi Paul Adams, *The First American Constitutions: Republican Ideology and the Making of the State Constitutions in the Revolutionary Era* (Chapel Hill: University of North Carolina Press, 1980), p. 18.

22. See Forrest McDonald, *Novus Ordo Seclorum: The Intellectual Origins of the Constitution* (Lawrence: University Press of Kansas, 1985), pp. 81–85, 209–13.

23. Zoltan Horaszti, *John Adams and the Prophets of Progress* (New York: Grosset and Dunlap, 1964), p. 28.

24. See Gordon Wood, *The Creation of the American Republic, 1776–1787* (Chapel Hill: University of North Carolina Press, 1969), p. 11: "No Government that ever existed, was so essentially free." See also pp. 575–86. Adams is quoted as saying in 1775 that the "British constitution is nothing more nor less than a republic, in which the king is first magistrate" (p. 206).

25. James Madison, *Notes of Debates in the Federal Convention of 1787* (Athens: Ohio University Press, 1966), p. 447. Madison quotes Dickinson as declaring, "It was not Reason that Discovered [this mechanism]." Experience takes the place of reason.

26. Ibid., p. 184.

27. Ibid., p. 46.

28. McDonald, *Novus Ordo Seclorum*, p. 209. In James Madison, no. 56 of *The Federalist*, ed. Jacob E. Cooke (Middletown, Conn.: Wesleyan University Press, 1961), p. 382, Madison speaks of the "experience of Great Britain which presents to mankind so many political lessons . . . [as] frequently consulted in the course of these inquiries."

29. See William Henry Drayton, *A Letter from Freeman of South Carolina to Deputies of North America, Assembled in the High Court of Congress in Philadelphia* (Charlestown: Peter Timothy, 1774), pp. 20, 24: "Magna Carta is such a fellow that he will have no other sovereign." See also Stephen D. White, *Sir Edward Coke and the "Grievances of the Commonwealth, 1621–1628"* (Chapel Hill: University of North Carolina Press, 1979), p. 267. The quotation is an echo of debates in the Parliament of 1628 leading up to the Petition of Right.

30. For a comparison of royal and republican executives in Madison's *Notes*, see James Wilson, pp. 46, 252, 444; Pierce Butler, pp. 63, 113; Gouverneur Morris, pp. 319, 335–36, 360, 373; George Mason, p. 64; Benjamin Franklin, p. 64; James Madison, pp. 80, 305; and Roger Sherman, p. 527. For a sample of analogies to Parliament, see George Mason, pp. 177, 252; Gunning Bedford, p. 229; and Roger Sherman, p. 399.

31. Madison, *Notes*, p. 82; the same comparison is made by Oliver Ellsworth (p. 223), Edmund Randolph (p. 436), and George Mason (p. 443).

32. Ellis Sandoz, "The American Constitutional Order After Two Centuries: Concluding Reflections," *Social Science Quarterly* 68 (December 1987): 724–44.

33. Elliot, *Debates*, 3:170, 174.

34. Ibid., pp. 53–54.

35. Ibid., pp. 450–51, 219. Henry Lee argues that since Parliament can contend with a king, Congress will be able to prevent executive tyranny (p. 43).

36. Ibid., 4:354.

37. George C. Rogers, Jr., *Evolution of a Federalist: William Loughton Smith of Charleston, 1758–1812* (Columbia: University of South Carolina Press, 1962), pp. 157–58.

38. Sir William Holdsworth, *The History of English Law*, 17 vols. (London: Methuen and Co., 1938), 11:137. Holdsworth adds that talk of the "equality of men, their inalienable rights . . . , [though] such theories might be suited to a period of revolution, [was] of very little help in a period of reconstruction." See also Sir William Blackstone, *Commentaries on the Laws of England*, 4 vols. (Chicago: Uni-

versity of Chicago Press, 1979), 1:91, 237, for an idea of the British constitution contrary to the one suggested in Dr. Bonham's case. Blackstone declares, "if the parliament will positively enact a thing to be done which is unreasonable, I know no power that can control it." Yet he denies that Parliament is free to exercise a "power precarious and impracticable."

39. Kammen, *A Machine That Would Go of Itself*, pp. 156–84; especially A. V. Dicey, Lord Acton, Walter Bagehot, Sir Henry Lunn, Lord Bryce, and William E. H. Lecky.

40. Michael Oakeshott, *On Human Conduct* (Oxford: Clarendon Press, 1975), pp. 201–3.

3. The Process of Ratification

1. On the Constitutional Convention as "theater," see my "Such a Government as the People Will Approve: The Great Convention as Comic Action," *St. Louis University Public Law Review* 6, no. 2 (Spring 1987): 215–28. It appears here as Chapter 1.

2. Recorded in James Madison, *Notes of Debates in the Federal Convention of 1787* (Athens: Ohio University Press, 1966), p. 74.

3. For my reading of ratification in South Carolina, see "Preserving the Birthright: The Intention of South Carolina in Adopting the United States Constitution," *South Carolina Historical Magazine* 89, no. 2 (Spring 1988): 30–41; for my commentary on the same process in the Bay State, see "A Dike to Fence Out the Flood: The Ratification of the Constitution in Massachusetts," *Chronicles* 11 (December 1987): 16–18, 20–23. Both of these essays are reprinted in this book, as Chapters 5 and 4.

4. See John P. Kaminski, "New York: The Reluctant Pillar," in *The Reluctant Pillar: New York and the Adoption of the Federal Constitution*, ed. Stephen L. Schechter (Troy, N.Y.: Russell Sage College, 1985), p. 114.

5. See *The Debates in the Several State Conventions on the Adoption of the Federal Constitution as Recommended by the General Convention at Philadelphia in 1787*, ed. Jonathan Elliot, 5 vols. (New York: J. B. Lippincott, 1876), 2:114, 3:649, 4:57.

6. Elliot, *Debates*, 4:330.

7. Ibid., 2:78.

8. Ibid., 2:131.

4. A Dike to Fence Out the Flood

1. *Debates and Proceedings in the Convention of the Commonwealth of Massachusetts, Held in the Year 1788, and Which Finally Ratified the Constitution of the United States* (Boston: William White, 1856). This volume contains material not printed elsewhere.

2. Samuel Bannister Harding, *The Contest over the Ratification of the Federal Constitution in the State of Massachusetts* (New York: Longmans, Green, and Co., 1896).

3. Van Beck Hall, *Politics Without Parties: Massachusetts, 1780–1791* (Pittsburgh: University of Pittsburgh Press, 1972); Robert Allen Rutland, *The Ordeal of the Constitution: The Antifederalists and the Ratification Struggle of 1787–1788* (Norman: University of Oklahoma Press, 1965), pp. 66–114.

4. Stephen E. Patterson, "The Roots of Massachusetts Federalism: Conservative Political Culture Before 1787," in *Sovereign States in an Age of Uncertainty*, ed. Ronald Hoffman and Peter S. Albert (Charlottesville: University Press of Virginia, 1981), pp. 31–61; James M. Banner, Jr., *To The Hartford Convention: The Federalists and the Origins of Party Politics in Massachusetts, 1789–1815* (New York: Alfred A. Knopf, 1970); Charles Warren, "Elbridge Gerry, James Warren, Mercy Warren, and the Ratification of the Federal Constitution in Massachusetts," *Massachusetts Historical Society Proceedings* 64 (1932): 143–64; Robert A. Feer, "Shays's Rebellion and the Constitution: A Study in Causation," *New England Quarterly* 42 (1969): 388–410; David P. Szatmary, *Shays' Rebellion: The Making of an Agrarian Insurrection* (Amherst: University of Massachusetts Press, 1980); and Richard O. Brown, "Shays's Rebellion and the Ratification of the Constitution in Massachusetts," in *Beyond Confederation: Origins of the Constitution and American National Identity*, ed. Richard Beeman, Stephen Botein, and Edward C. Carter II (Chapel Hill: University of North Carolina Press, 1987), pp. 113–27.

5. *Debates and Proceedings*, p. 246, where the Reverend Thomas Thacher observes that in Europe "American faith is a proverbial expression for perfidy, as punic faith was among the Romans."

6. Harding, *The Contest over Ratification*, p. 12.

7. *Debates and Proceedings*, p. 107; though at other times Ames embraces a version of natural rights theory, he does not do so in the ratification convention.

8. Ibid., p. 249.

9. Ibid., pp. 107, 130, 203, 318.

10. Ibid., p. 260.

11. Ibid., p. 295.

12. The first quotation is from John P. Kaminski, "Democracy Run Rampant:

Rhode Island in the Confederation," in *The Human Dimension of Nation Making: Essays on Colonial and Revolutionary America*, ed. James Kirby Martin (Madison: State Historical Society of Wisconsin, 1976), p. 261; the second from Lynn Turner, *William Plumer of New Hampshire, 1759–1850* (Chapel Hill: University of North Carolina Press, 1962), p. 21; the third from a Henry Knox letter to George Washington quoted in James T. Flexner, *George Washington and the New Nation: 1783–1793* (Boston: Little, Brown, 1970), p. 99.

13. Such alarms are also sounded in Antifederalist pamphlets and newspaper essays from Massachusetts. See volume 4 of *The Complete Anti-Federalist*, ed. Herbert J. Storing (Chicago: University of Chicago Press, 1981).

14. *Debates and Proceedings*, p. 187.

15. Ibid., p. 178.

16. Ibid., p. 265; see also Banner, *To the Hartford Convention*, p. 63.

17. Richard E. Welch, Jr., *Theodore Sedgwick, Federalist: A Political Portrait* (Middletown, Conn.: Wesleyan University Press, 1966), p. 60.

18. *Debates and Proceedings*, p. 233.

19. See Harding, *The Contest over Ratification*, p. 1.

20. Brown, "Shays's Rebellion," p. 127; Bradford K. Pierce and Charles Hale, eds., preface to *Debates and Proceedings*, p. iii; and Jackson Turner Main, *The Antifederalists: Critics of the Constitution, 1781–1787* (Chapel Hill: University of North Carolina Press, 1961), p. 200.

21. Elbridge Gerry, who had been an Antifederalist inside the Great Convention, was asked to sit with the Massachusetts ratification convention as a source of information but left in anger when not allowed to speak.

22. Brown, "Shays's Rebellion," p. 127.

23. *Debates and Proceedings*, p. 169.

24. Ibid., p. 291.

25. Ibid., pp. 217 and 139.

26. Ibid., pp. 301 and 320.

27. Ibid., p. 303.

28. Ibid., p. 251.

29. Ibid., p. 310; also Hall, *Politics Without Parties*, p. 281.

30. *Debates and Proceedings*, p. 169.

31. Ibid.; p. 228.

32. See Forrest McDonald, *We the People: The Economic Origins of the Constitution* (Chicago: University of Chicago Press, 1958), pp. 184–85; also Rutland, *The Ordeal of the Constitution*, p. 106.

33. *Debates and Proceedings*, pp. 79–80.

34. Brown, "Shays's Rebellion," p. 126.
35. *Debates and Proceedings*, pp. 113, 235, and 240.
36. Ibid., pp. 102 and 262.
37. Ibid., p. 203.
38. Ibid., p. 293.
39. Ibid., p. 181.
40. Ibid., pp. 201–2.
41. Ibid., p. 303.
42. Ibid., p. 132.
43. Ibid., p. 204.
44. Ibid., pp. 203 and 205.
45. Ibid., p. 275.
46. Banner, *To the Hartford Convention*, pp. 84–91.
47. *Debates and Proceedings*, p. 264.
48. Ibid., p. 152.
49. Ibid., p. 253.
50. Ibid., p. 109.
51. Ibid., pp. 307 and 143.
52. Ibid., p. 261.
53. Ibid., p. 262.
54. Ibid., pp. 105–6.
55. Ibid., p. 205.
56. Ibid.

57. All of this teaching is reflected in the doctrine of Theophilus Parsons, who maintained that there are no absolutely inalienable rights because the welfare of an entire society cannot permit (or should not be put at risk by) such a presumption of anterior imperatives. His position on natural rights was commonplace in the thought of many New England Federalists. See Banner, *To the Hartford Convention*, p. 63, for an analysis of Parsons's position on "rights" in the Essex Resolves. In the Massachusetts ratification convention, Antifederalists made most of the appeals to a theory of presocial rights.

58. Banner, *To the Hartford Convention*, p. 59.

59. Those joined in the Mayflower Compact of 11 November 1620 agree to act "as shall be thought right for the general good of the colony unto which we promise all due submission and obedience."

60. See *The Debates in the Several State Conventions on the Adoption of the Federal Constitution as Recommended by the General Convention at Philadelphia in 1787*, ed. Jonathan Elliot, 5 vols. (New York: J. B. Lippincott, 1876), 3:259 and 620.

5. *Preserving the Birthright*

1. James Madison, *Notes of Debates in the Federal Convention of 1787* (Athens: Ohio University Press, 1966), p. 74.

2. *The Debates in the Several State Conventions on the Adoption of the Federal Constitution as Recommended by the General Convention at Philadelphia in 1787*, ed. Jonathan Elliot, 5 vols. (New York: J. B. Lippincott, 1876), 4:315–16. An interesting illustration of South Carolina's distrust of abstractions appears in the "Introduction" to *Journals of the House of Representatives, 1787–1788* (Columbia: University of South Carolina Press, 1981), pp. xiii–xiv. There we read of Speaker John Julius Pringle's censure of David Ramsay's argument from definition against violations of the law of contract. Pringle's answer was that "no contract was sacred," that the law of contracts could not be put above the good of society. He pleads for the common good: "The safety of the people is the law paramount, to which every other must yield." For the history of South Carolina in the years prior to the ratification convention, see Charles Gregg Singer, *South Carolina in the Confederation* (Philadelphia: Porcupine Press, 1941).

3. Elliot, *Debates*, 4:311.

4. See Richard Brent Clow, "Edward Rutledge of South Carolina, 1749–1800: Unproclaimed Statesman" (Ph.D. diss., University of Georgia, 1976), p. 105.

5. See letter of Edward Rutledge to John Jay, 19 June 1776, reprinted in Clow, "Rutledge of South Carolina," p. 99.

6. Elliot, *Debates*, 4:272. Here Lowndes echoes what John Rutledge himself argues in the Great Convention—that the question of slavery had to do with "interests" and nothing more. See Madison, *Notes*, p. 502.

7. What is maintained about slavery in the ratification conventions is inconsistent and sporadic. General Nathan Miller of Rhode Island, a Federalist, also treats the institution as a positive good. See *Theodore Foster's Minutes of the Convention Held at South Kingston, Rhode Island in March 1790, Which Failed to Adopt the Constitution of the United States*, transcribed and annotated by Robert C. Cotner (Providence: Rhode Island Historical Society, 1929), pp. 36, 50–52. Most Antifederalists in New York were proslavery. In Connecticut some Antifederalists were antislavery. See the speech of Benjamin Gale ostensibly given at Killingworth, Connecticut, on 12 November 1787, printed in vol. 3 of *The Documentary History of the Ratification of the Constitution by the States: Delaware, New Jersey, Georgia, Connecticut*, ed. Merrill Jensen, 19 vols. (Madison: State Historical Society of Wisconsin, 1978), pp. 420–29. The same is true of Pennsylvania and Massachusetts. In Virginia, Zachariah Johnson, a frontier Federalist, predicts emancipation (Elliot, *Debates*, 3:648),

while most of the Federalists say it cannot happen. In Maryland, Luther Martin, an Antifederalist, spoke severely of the trade to an indifferent convention. Yet there is no pattern, nor any proof of a settled attitude on the subject. The best conclusion is that a majority of the Framers were not greatly concerned with slavery.

8. Elliot, *Debates*, 4:272.

9. Ibid., p. 274.

10. Ibid., p. 262.

11. Ibid., pp. 271–72.

12. Ibid., pp. 310–11.

13. Ibid., p. 271.

14. Ibid., p. 287.

15. Ibid., p. 282.

16. Ibid., p. 302.

17. Ibid., pp. 286 and 316.

18. Ibid., p. 259. Charles Pinckney argues here what James Madison is soon to say in Virginia (Elliot, *Debates*, 3:620), and James Iredell in North Carolina (4:102 and 171–72).

19. Ibid., 4:276.

20. Ibid., p. 287.

21. Ibid., p. 289.

22. Ibid., p. 273. See also Francis Bowen, *Life of Benjamin Lincoln* (Boston: C. Little and J. Brown, 1855).

23. Elliot, *Debates*, 4:310.

24. Ibid., p. 274.

25. Ibid., p. 272.

26. Quoted from John Drayton, *Memoirs of the American Revolution, from Its Commencement to the Year 1776*, 2 vols. (Charleston: A. E. Miller, 1821), 1:254–60.

27. Elliot, *Debates*, 4:337. On Dollard's life, see vol. 3 of *Biographical Directory of the South Carolina House of Representatives*, ed. Louise Bailey and Elizabeth Ivy Cooper, 3 vols. (Columbia: University of South Carolina Press, 1981), p. 188. General reports of the ratification debates not printed by Elliot appeared in the Charleston *City Gazette* or the *Daily Advertiser*.

28. See George C. Rogers, Jr., *Evolution of a Federalist: William Loughton Smith of Charleston, 1758–1812* (Columbia: University of South Carolina Press, 1962), pp. 169–70.

29. George C. Rogers, Jr., "South Carolina Ratifies the Federal Constitution," *South Carolina Historical Proceedings* (1961): 41–62. See Jerome J. Nadelhaft, *The*

Disorders of War: The Revolution in South Carolina (Orono: University of Maine Press, 1981), pp. 173–90. See also Raymond G. Starr, "The Conservative Revolution: South Carolina Public Affairs, 1775–1790" (Ph.D. diss., University of Texas, 1964), pp. 251–62; and especially Forrest McDonald, *We the People: The Economic Origins of the Constitution* (Chicago: University of Chicago Press, 1958), pp. 202–35.

30. Quoted from *The Making of the American Republic: The Great Documents, 1774–1789*, ed. Charles Callan Tansill (New Rochelle, N.Y.: Arlington House, 1972), p. 1023.

6. A Great Refusal

1. For the records of the Hillsborough Convention, see *The Debates in the Several State Conventions on the Adoption of the Federal Constitution as Recommended by the General Convention at Philadelphia in 1787*, ed. Jonathan Elliot, 5 vols. (New York: J. B. Lippincott, 1876), 4:1–252. I cite here Elliot, *Debates*, 4:25–51.

2. The standard authorities on ratification in North Carolina are Louise Irby Trenholme, *The Ratification of the Federal Constitution in North Carolina* (New York: Columbia University Press, 1932), and A. R. Newsome, "North Carolina's Ratification of the Federal Constitution," *North Carolina Historical Review* 17 (October 1940): 287–301. For the best of recent essays on the subject, see Alan D. Watson, "North Carolina: States' Rights and Agrarianism Ascendant," in *The Constitution and the States: The Role of the Original Thirteen in the Framing and Adoption of the Federal Constitution*, ed. Patrick T. Conley and John P. Kaminski (Madison, Wisc.: Madison House, 1988), pp. 251–68; and J. Edwin Hendricks, "Joining the Federal Union," in *The North Carolina Experience*, ed. Lindley S. Butler and Alan D. Watson (Chapel Hill: University of North Carolina Press, 1984), pp. 147–57. For a valuable discussion of North Carolina's second ratification convention, which approved the United States Constitution, see John C. Cavanagh, *Decision at Fayetteville: The North Carolina Ratification Convention and General Assembly of 1789* (Raleigh: Division of Archives and History, North Carolina Department of Cultural Resources, 1989).

3. On the importance of sequence in the dynamic of ratification, see my essay "The Process of Ratification: A Study of Political Dynamics," first published in *Chronicles* 15, no. 2 (February 1991): 18–20. A longer version of this essay appears as Chapter 3 in this book.

4. Elliot, *Debates*, 4:4. There is need for a detailed study of Willie Jones. The best we have is Blackwell P. Robinson, "Willie Jones of Halifax" (parts 1 and 2),

North Carolina Historical Review 18 (April 1941): 1–26, and (July 1941): 133–70.

5. Elliot, *Debates*, 4:15.

6. Ibid., p. 7.

7. Ibid., p. 8.

8. Ibid., p. 13.

9. See vol. 1 of *The Records of the Federal Convention of 1787*, ed. Max Farrand (New Haven: Yale University Press, 1937), pp. 26–27. The cited passage appears in the notes of James McHenry for 29 May 1787.

10. Elliot, *Debates*, 4:244.

11. Ibid., p. 53.

12. Ibid., p. 195.

13. Ibid., p. 160.

14. Ibid., p. 148. Iredell is consistent and persuasive in representing himself as a very mild Federalist. His behavior as a justice of the United States Supreme Court indicates that he was not posturing when he spoke this way in Hillsborough.

15. Elliot, *Debates*, 4:188.

16. Ibid., pp. 50 and 34. Maclaine, Iredell, and Davie (as did Madison in Virginia) represent the new government as being only "a little stronger" than what the Antifederalists are ready to accept.

17. Elliot, *Debates*, 4:55.

18. Ibid., p. 102.

19. Ibid., p. 29.

20. Ibid., pp. 231 and 238.

21. Ibid., p. 240.

22. Ibid., p. 35.

23. Ibid., p. 126.

24. Ibid., p. 35.

25. Ibid., p. 37.

26. Ibid., p. 36.

27. Trenholme, *The Ratification of the Federal Constitution in North Carolina*, p. 168.

28. Elliot, *Debates*, 4:51.

29. Ibid., p. 57.

30. Ibid., p. 90. The connection between economic interests and political position among the delegates to the Hillsborough Convention is explored by William C. Pool in "An Economic Interpretation of the Ratification of the Federal Constitution in North Carolina," *North Carolina Historical Review* 27 (April 1950): 119–41, (July 1950): 289–313, and (October 1950): 437–61.

31. Elliot, *Debates*, 4:24.

32. Ibid., p. 212.

33. Ibid., p. 115.

34. Ibid., p. 102.

35. Ibid., p. 176.

36. Ibid., p. 124.

37. Ibid., pp. 152 and 163.

38. Ibid., p. 180.

39. Ibid., p. 179.

40. Ibid., p. 160.

41. Ibid., p. 163. For the theory that the first North Carolina ratification convention was a dispute between two disparate conceptions of law, see William F. Pratt, Jr., "Law and the Experience of Politics in Late Eighteenth-Century North Carolina: North Carolina Considers the Constitution," *Wake Forest Law Review* 22 (1987): 577–605. See also Elliot, *Debates*, 4:162.

42. Elliot, *Debates*, 4:191–215, for the entire discussion.

43. Ibid., pp. 191–92.

44. Ibid., p. 195.

45. Ibid., p. 196.

46. Ibid., p. 200.

47. Ibid., p. 95.

48. Ibid., p. 219.

49. Watson, "North Carolina: States' Rights and Agrarianism Ascendant," p. 263.

50. Elliot, *Debates*, 4:69; see also Judge Iredell in Elliot, *Debates*, 4:14.

51. Ibid., p. 51.

52. Ibid., p. 93.

53. Ibid., p. 243.

54. See Hendricks, "Joining the Federal Union," pp. 148–49.

55. Limited government in the context means of necessity no federal protection for individual rights except by way of such limitation. The Constitution modifies this formula with a few discrete protections (against bills of attainder, violations of copyright, denial of trial by jury, etc.) but offers nothing generic.

56. Elliot, *Debates*, 4:123.

57. I refer here to the extraordinary (but unpersuasive) essay by Michael Lienesch entitled "North Carolina: Preserving Rights," in *Ratifying the Constitution*, ed. Michael Allen Gillespie and Michael Lienesch (Lawrence: University Press of Kansas, 1989), pp. 343–67.

58. Lienesch emphasizes the change rather than the continuity of American politics marked by the ratification of our Constitution.

7. Religion and the Framers

1. I here draw upon only a very small selection of the evidence available in the wills written by the Framers. For my account of the Philadelphia Framers, see *A Worthy Company: Brief Lives of the Framers of the United States Constitution* (Marlborough, N.H.: Plymouth Rock Foundation, 1982).

2. Norine Dickson Campbell, *Patrick Henry: Patriot and Statesman* (New York: Devin-Adair Co., 1969), p. 272.

3. Ibid., p. 418.

4. William Jay, *The Life of John Jay with Selections from His Correspondence*, 3 vols. (New York: Harper, 1833), 1:519–20.

5. *The Papers of George Mason, 1725–1792*, ed. Robert A. Rutland, 3 vols. (Chapel Hill: University of North Carolina Press, 1970), 1:147.

6. *The Papers of William Livingston*, ed. Carl E. Prince, 5 vols. (Trenton: New Jersey Historical Commission, 1979–88), 1:43–44.

7. David John Mays, *Edmund Pendleton, 1721–1803*, 2 vols. (Cambridge: Harvard University Press, 1952), 1:357.

8. See Oliver Perry Chitwood, *Richard Henry Lee: Statesman of the Revolution* (Morgantown: West Virginia University Library, 1967).

9. See Christopher Collier, *Roger Sherman's Connecticut: Yankee Politics and the American Revolution* (Middletown, Conn.: Wesleyan University Press, 1971); see also William Garrott Brown, *The Life of Oliver Ellsworth* (New York: Da Capo Press, 1970), pp. 330–31; M. E. Bradford, "The Maryland Vesuvius: The Politics of Samuel Chase," *Southern Partisan* 6 (Summer 1986): 40–44; M. E. Bradford, "Caleb Strong," in *A Worthy Company*, pp. 16–17; and M. E. Bradford, "High Federalist Teaching: Theodore Sedgwick of Massachusetts," *Intercollegiate Review* 25 (Spring 1990): 31–37.

10. George Adams Boyd, *Elias Boudinot: Patriot and Statesman, 1740–1821* (Princeton: Princeton University Press, 1952).

11. Collier, *Roger Sherman's Connecticut*, pp. 325–29.

12. Marvin R. Zahniser, *Charles Cotesworth Pinckney: Founding Father* (Chapel Hill: University of North Carolina Press, 1967), pp. 272–74.

13. Milton E. Fowler, *John Dickinson: Conservative Revolutionary* (Charlottesville: University Press of Virginia, 1983), p. 287.

14. For the passage from Morris, see Max M. Mintz, *Gouverneur Morris and the American Revolution* (Norman: University of Oklahoma Press, 1970), p. 127; on Hamilton's dying request, see Broadus Mitchell, *Alexander Hamilton: A Concise Biography* (New York: Oxford University Press, 1976), pp.373–74.

15. See *The Debates in the Several State Conventions on the Adoption of the Federal Constitution as Recommended by the General Convention at Philadelphia in 1787*, ed. Jonathan Elliot, 5 vols (New York: J. B. Lippincott, 1876), 2:202.

16. Elliot, *Debates*, 4:196.

17. *The Annals of the Congress of the United States: The Debates and Proceedings in the Congress of the United States*, compiled from authentic materials by Joseph Gales, Senior, 34 vols. (Washington: Gales and Seaton, 1834), 1:729–31.

18. Our first amendment was actually the third in a list of twelve sent out for approval by the states.

19. See Robert Allen Rutland, *The Birth of the Bill of Rights, 1776–1791* (Chapel Hill: University of North Carolina Press, 1955), especially pp. 214–16; see also vol. 1 of *Documentary History of the First Federal Congress of the United States of America*, ed. Linda Grant De Pauw (Baltimore: Johns Hopkins University Press, 1972).

20. Michael J. Malbin, *Religion and Politics: The Intentions of the Authors of the First Amendment* (Washington, D.C.: American Enterprise Institute, 1978), p. 20.

21. See *The Founders' Constitution*, ed. Philip B. Kurland and Ralph Lerner, 5 vols. (Chicago: University of Chicago Press, 1987), 5:93.

22. Elliot, *Debates*, 4:195; also 3:330 (by Madison himself).

23. *Theodore Foster's Minutes of the Convention Held at South Kingston, Rhode Island in March 1790, Which Failed to Adopt the Constitution of the United States*, transcribed and annotated by Robert C. Cotner (Providence: Rhode Island Historical Society, 1929), p. 58.

24. Thomas J. Curry, *The First Freedoms: Church and State in America to the Passage of the First Amendment* (New York: Oxford University Press, 1987).

25. James McClellan, "The Making and Unmaking of the Establishment Clause," in *A Blueprint for Judicial Reform*, ed. Patrick B. McGuigan and Randall R. Rader (Washington, D.C.: Free Congress Foundation, 1981), p. 306; see also John Francis Thorning, *Religious Liberty in Transition* (Washington, D.C.: Catholic University of America Press, 1931), p. 27; and Philip B. Kurland, "The Irrelevance of the Constitution: The Religion Clauses of the First Amendment and the Supreme Court," *Villanova Law Review* 24 (1978–79): 3–21.

26. *The Eighteenth-Century Constitution: Documents and Commentary, 1688–1815*, ed. E. N. Williams (Cambridge: Cambridge University Press, 1960), pp. 325–48.

27. McClellan, "The Establishment Clause," p. 307.

28. Malbin, *Religion and Politics*, p. 9. For a contrasting view, see Father Curry's teacher, Leonard W. Levy, *The Establishment Clause: Religion and the First Amendment* (New York: Macmillan, 1986), a tendentious book written by a man who dislikes the world of the Fathers of the Republic and therefore misrepresents it.

29. Mark DeWolfe Howe, *The Garden and the Wilderness: Religion and Government in American Constitutional History* (Chicago: University of Chicago Press, 1965), pp. 4, 22–23, 31; also Robert L. Cord, *Separation of Church and State: Historical Fact and Current Fiction* (New York: Lambeth Press, 1982), pp. 26–29; also Wilbur Katz, *Religion and the American Constitutions* (Evanston, Ill.: Northwestern University Press, 1964); and Edward S. Corwin, *A Constitution of Powers in a Secular State* (Charlottesville, Va.: Michie Co., 1951).

30. In this long and quiet history *Reynolds v. United States*, 98 U.S. 145 (1878), the polygamy case, is anomalous.

31. Kurland and Lerner, *The Founders' Constitution*, 5:94.

32. See Stephen Botein, "Religious Dimensions of the Early American State," in *Beyond Confederation: Origins of the Constitution and American National Identity*, ed. Richard Beeman, Stephen Botein, and Edward C. Carter II (Chapel Hill: University of North Carolina Press, 1987), pp. 315–30.

33. Curry, *The First Freedoms*, 216–19.

34. See the minority opinion in *Wallace v. Jaffree*, 105 S. Ct. 2479, 2505 (1984).

8. *Changed Only a Little*

1. The substantive rights decisions following upon the Supreme Court's ruling in *Lochner v. New York*, 198 U.S. 45 (1905), could perhaps be taken as a third exception; however, these cases are actually only a subset of the pattern of inventive construction under investigation in this chapter.

2. For discussion of the constitutional morality of these "limited government" Republicans and of their devotion to a very restricted federalism, see Phillip S. Paludan, *A Covenant with Death: The Constitution, Law, and Equality in the Civil War Era* (Urbana: University of Illinois Press, 1975), especially pp. 274–82; Michael L. Benedict, "Preserving the Constitution: The Conservative Basis of Radical Reconstruction," *Journal of American History* 61 (1974): 65–90; Herman Belz, *A New Birth of Freedom: The Republican Party and Freedman's Rights, 1861–1866* (Westport, Conn.: Greenwood Press, 1976); Herman Belz, *Emancipation and Equal Rights: Politics and Constitutionalism in the Civil War Era* (New York: Norton, 1978); Daniel

Elazar, "The Civil War and the Preservation of Federalism," *Publius* 1 (1970): 39–58; Charles Fairman, *Reconstruction and Reunion, 1864–1888*, part 1, vol. 6 of *The Oliver Wendell Holmes Devise, History of the Supreme Court of the United States* (New York: Macmillan, 1971); Charles Fairman, *Reconstruction and Reunion, 1864–1888*, part 2, vol. 7 of *The Oliver Wendell Holmes Devise, History of the Supreme Court of the United States* (New York: Macmillan, 1987); Bernard Schwartz, *From Confederation to Nation, 1835–1877* (Baltimore: Johns Hopkins University Press, 1973); Raoul Berger, *Government by Judiciary: The Transformation of the Fourteenth Amendment* (Cambridge: Harvard University Press, 1971); Michael L. Benedict, *A Compromise of Principle: Congressional Republicans and Reconstruction, 1863–1869* (New York: Norton, 1974); Alfred Avins, "The Equal Protection of the Laws: The Original Understanding," *New York Law Forum* 12 (1967): 385–429; Alfred Avins, "The Civil Rights Law of 1875: Some Reflected Light on the Fourteenth Amendment and Public Accommodations," *Columbia Law Review* 66 (1966): 873–915; and Earl Maltz, "Reconstruction Without Revolution: Republican Civil Rights Theory in the Era of the Fourteenth Amendment," *Houston Law Review* 24 (1987): 231–66.

3. Philip B. Kurland, "The Constitutional Impact of Public Policy: From the Warren Court to the Burger Court and Beyond," *World and I* 1, no. 8 (August 1986): 582, 583.

4. Russell Kirk, "The Constitution of the United States Was Not Written by Locke," *World and I* 1, no. 11 (November 1986): 568, 571.

5. Willmoore Kendall, "Equality: Commitment or Ideal?" *Intercollegiate Review* 24 (Spring 1989): 25–33; also Willmoore Kendall and George W. Carey, *The Basic Symbols of the American Political Tradition* (Baton Rouge: Louisiana State University Press, 1970), pp. 94–156.

6. Forrest McDonald, *Novus Ordo Seclorum: The Intellectual Origins of the Constitution* (Lawrence: University Press of Kansas, 1985), pp. 292–93.

7. Ibid., p. 67.

8. Michael Oakeshott, *On Human Conduct* (Oxford: Clarendon Press, 1975); "Talking Politics," *National Review* 27 (5 December, 1975): 1345–47, 1423–28.

9. Michael Oakeshott, *On History and Other Essays* (Oxford: Basil Blackwell, 1983), pp. 119–64.

10. Ibid., pp. 139 and 143.

11. Ibid., p. 139.

12. Oakeshott, *On Human Conduct*, pp. 199–206.

13. Oakeshott, *On History and Other Essays*, pp. 155–88.

14. The Reconstruction Acts of 1867 and 1868 are also part of this pattern.

15. Senator Lyman Trumbull, Senator Reverdy Johnson, Professor Thomas

Cooley, Judge John Norton Pomeroy, Professor Joel Parker, Justice Samuel Miller, Chief Justice Morrison Waite (1874–88), and many others. Their thought is examined in Paludan's *A Covenant with Death*.

16. I refer here to the obvious sectional quality of the Voting Rights Act of 1965, and its sequels, which make reference to (and, in function, turn upon) voting patterns in an earlier time: practices measured by their impact, probably legal when they occurred.

17. See Berger, *Government by Judiciary*, pp. 230–45. For neoabolitionist jurisprudence, see Jacobus tenBroek, *Equal Under Law* (New York: Collier Books, 1965); Howard Jay Graham, *Everyman's Constitution* (New York: Norton, 1968); Robert J. Kaczorowski, *The Politics of Judicial Interpretation: The Federal Courts, Department of Justice, and Civil Rights, 1866–1876* (Dobbs Ferry, N.Y.: Oceana, 1985); Michael Kent Curtis, *No State Shall Abridge: The Fourteenth Amendment and the Bill of Rights* (Durham: Duke University Press, 1986); and Robert J. Kaczorowski, "To Begin the Nation Anew: Congress, Citizenship, and Civil Rights After the Civil War," *American Historical Review* 92 (1987): 45–68.

18. See Harold M. Hyman and William M. Wiecek, *Equal Justice Under Law: Constitutional Development, 1835–1875* (New York: Harper and Row, 1982)—a refinement of the tradition of neoabolitionist historiography, an impressive though highly partisan work, filled with the combination of "thoroughness" and "passion" that its authors admire in the "tendentious Dwight L. Dumond of the University of Michigan" (p. 539). See also pp. 492 and 507, where Hyman and Wiecek speak of the incorporative quality of the Thirteenth Amendment. On p. 552 Hyman and Wiecek refer to the opposing view of their subject, the interpretivist approach to strict construction of the Constitution, as having been "buried at Gettysburg and Appomattox"—after having expended a massive effort to prevent its resurrection from the dead.

19. See Hyman and Wiecek, *Equal Justice Under Law*, p. 389.

20. David Donald, *Charles Sumner and the Rights of Man* (New York: Alfred A. Knopf, 1970), pp. 149–50.

21. See Fairman, *Reconstruction and Reunion*, part 1, vol. 6, pp. 1157, 1236. I cite from both Henderson and Senator Thomas A. Hendricks of Indiana.

22. Ibid., p. 1159. Passage of the Civil Rights Act of 1866 depended on the support of men who did not accept abolitionist and radical constitutional theory.

23. Donald, *Charles Sumner and the Rights of Man*, p. 151.

24. Ibid., p. 532.

25. One useful indication of the limited purpose of the Thirteenth Amendment appears in a letter written by Secretary of State Seward in which he insists that

section 2 of the amendment "is really restraining in its effect, instead of enlarging the powers of Congress." See Schwartz, *From Confederation to Nation*, p. 194. Fairman quotes from several senators and congressmen (Democrats and conservative Republicans) who felt that the amendment settled nothing about the future status of the freedman. His conclusion is that they would not have the amendment had they believed it would "impose the peculiar doctrines of the most radical among them" (i.e., in the Congress) on the states. See Fairman, *Reconstruction and Reunion*, part 1, vol. 6, pp. 1157–59.

26. Fairman, *Reconstruction and Reunion*, part 1, vol. 6, p. 1156. It is true, however, that the Thirteenth Amendment made it easier to attempt to increase the supervisory power of the general government, even though its adoption "introduces no intricate question of constitutional law." Before 1860 such a revision would have been unthinkable.

27. Hyman and Wiecek, *Equal Justice Under Law*, pp. 506–7.

28. Neoabolitionist historians cannot expect to find what they want in the amendment just because it has an enactment clause. It is a simple matter to explain the attachment of that clause as a measure designed merely to free the slaves when we remember how old slavery was in North America and the ferocity of the just concluded War Between the States.

29. See V. Jacque Voegeli, *Free but Not Equal: The Midwest and the Negro During the Civil War* (Chicago: University of Chicago Press, 1967), p. 176.

30. Quoted in Schwartz, *From Confederation to Nation*, p. 193.

31. Ibid., pp. 191–92.

32. Ibid., p. 208, the Enforcement Act of 1870.

33. Hyman and Wiecek, *Equal Justice Under Law*, p. 507.

34. See the discussion in Forrest G. Wood, *Black Scare: The Racist Response to Emancipation and Reconstruction* (Berkeley: University of California Press, 1970), pp. 156–69; also James M. McPherson, *The Struggle for Equality: Abolitionists and the Negro in the Civil War and Reconstruction* (Princeton: Princeton University Press, 1964), and *The Abolitionist Legacy* (Princeton: Princeton University Press, 1975), pp. 24–34.

35. LaWanda Cox and John Cox, *Politics, Principle, and Prejudice, 1865–1866* (New York: Atheneum, 1969) — a good example of their tendency to underestimate the strength of racial feeling in the North.

36. Schwartz, *From Confederation to Nation*, p. 216.

37. I quote Justice Joseph P. Bradley. See Fairman, *Reconstruction and Reunion*, part 1, vol. 6, p. 1362.

38. See in particular Senator Lyman Trumbull of Illinois and Senator Reverdy

Johnson of Maryland, in Fairman, *Reconstruction and Reunion*, part 1, vol. 6, pp. 1237 and 1180.

39. Fairman, *Reconstruction and Reunion*, part 1, vol. 6, p. 1218.

40. Ibid., p. 1228.

41. Ibid., p. 1253.

42. Ibid., p. 1216. For instruction in the political circumstances that prevented enactment of the protections for black rights which Justice Stewart imagines, see Voegeli, *Free but Not Equal*; McPherson, *The Abolitionist Legacy*; Eugene H. Berwanger, *The Frontier Against Slavery: Western Anti-Negro Prejudice and the Slavery Extension Controversy* (Urbana: University of Illinois Press, 1967); James A. Rawley, *Race and Politics: Bleeding Kansas and the Coming of the Civil War* (Philadelphia: J. B. Lippincott, 1969); George M. Fredrickson, *The Black Image in the White Mind: The Debate on Afro-American Character and Destiny, 1817–1914* (New York: Harper and Row, 1971); Leon F. Latwick, *Been in the Storm So Long: The Aftermath of Slavery* (New York: Random House, 1980); and William Gillette, *Retreat from Reconstruction, 1869–1879* (Baton Rouge: Louisiana State University Press, 1979).

43. Fairman, *Reconstruction and Reunion*, part 1, vol. 6, p. 1234.

44. Ibid., p. 1249. See also pp. 1238–44, where Fairman examines carefully the tortured logic of Justice Stewart in finding authority in the Fourteenth Amendment to restrain private or unofficial community action, using language concerning "custom" anachronistically.

45. Ibid., p. 1258.

46. See Fairman, *Reconstruction and Reunion*, part 2, p. 559.

47. See Charles Fairman, "Does the Fourteenth Amendment Incorporate the Bill of Rights?," in *The Fourteenth Amendment and the Bill of Rights: The Incorporation Theory*, ed. Leonard W. Levy (New York: Da Capo Press, 1970), p. 157. For related readings of this amendment, see Lino Graglia, "Do We Have an Unwritten Constitution? – The Privileges or Immunities Clause of the Fourteenth Amendment," *Harvard Journal of Law and Public Policy* 12 (1989): 84–89; and James McClellan, "The New Liberty of Contract Under the Thirteenth Amendment: The Case Against *Runyon* v. *McCrary*," *Benchmark* 3 (1987): 279–306.

48. See Felice A. Bonadio, *North of Reconstruction: Ohio Politics, 1865–1870* (New York: New York University Press, 1970), p. 85.

49. Berger, *Government by Judiciary*, pp. 194–98. See chapters 39 and 40 of Magna Carta, which became chapter 29 in the official Charter of Henry III (1224–25).

50. Ibid., p. 46.

51. Ibid., p. 103.

52. Ibid., pp. 46–48.

53. Ibid., pp. 46 and 48; also Hyman and Wiecek, *Equal Justice Under Law*, p. 477.

54. Fairman, *Reconstruction and Reunion*, part 1, vol. 6, p. 1352.

55. Berger, *Government by Judiciary*, p. 49.

56. Fairman, *Reconstruction and Reunion*, part 1, vol. 6, p. 1359.

57. Other important evidence supportive of a narrow view of the Fourteenth Amendment appears in two articles by Dean James E. Bond: "The Original Understanding of the Fourteenth Amendment in Illinois, Ohio, and Pennsylvania," *Akron Law Review* 18 (1985): 435–63; and "Ratification of the Fourteenth Amendment in North Carolina," *Wake Forest Law Review* 20 (1984): 89–119.

58. See Fawn M. Brodie, *Thaddeus Stevens: The Scourge of the South* (New York: Norton, 1966), p. 320; also Joseph B. James, *The Framing of the Fourteenth Amendment* (Urbana: University of Illinois Press, 1965), p. 201.

59. Berger, *Government by Judiciary*, p. 149. He quotes Senator James R. Doolittle of Wisconsin.

60. Donald, *Charles Sumner and the Rights of Man*, pp. 236–64.

61. Fairman, *Reconstruction and Reunion*, part 1, vol. 6, p. 1289. On Bingham, see also Berger, *Government by Judiciary*, pp. 145, 147, and Benedict, *A Compromise of Principle*, p. 170.

62. Berger, *Government by Judiciary*, pp. 157–65.

63. Ibid., p. 24.

64. Ibid., pp. 107–8; see also Alexander M. Bickel, *The Least Dangerous Branch* (Indianapolis: Bobbs-Merrill, 1962), p. 63.

65. Berger, *Government by Judiciary*, p. 387.

66. Ibid., p. 370; see also Leonard W. Levy, "Introduction" to *The Fourteenth Amendment and the Bill of Rights: The Incorporation Theory* (New York: Da Capo Press, 1970), p. xv.

67. Berger, *Government by Judiciary*, p. 393.

68. William Gillette, *The Right to Vote: Politics and the Passage of the Fifteenth Amendment* (Baltimore: Johns Hopkins University Press, 1965).

69. Bonadio, *North of Reconstruction*.

70. Schwartz, *From Confederation to Nation*, p. 206; see also Hyman and Wiecek, *Equal Justice Under Law*, p. 464.

71. Gillette, *Retreat from Reconstruction*, p. 19.

72. Ibid., p. 49.

73. Schwartz, *From Confederation to Nation*, pp. 212–13 and 216.

74. Gillette, *Retreat from Reconstruction*, p. 258.

75. Levy, *The Fourteenth Amendment and the Bill of Rights*, p. xv.

76. James Madison, *Notes of Debates in the Federal Convention of 1787* (Athens: Ohio University Press, 1966), p. 72.

Epilogue: The Comforting Delusion

1. See *The Founders' Constitution*, ed. Philip B. Kurland and Ralph Lerner, 5 vols. (Chicago: University of Chicago Press, 1987), 2:18. The passage is from Justice Joseph Story, *Commentaries on the Constitution of the United States*, 3 vols. (Boston: Hillard, Gray and Co., 1833).

2. Mortimer Adler, *We Hold These Truths: Understanding the Ideas and Ideals of the Constitution* (New York: Macmillan, 1987).

3. Ibid., p. 7.

4. Ibid., p. 159.

5. Philip B. Kurland, "The Constitutional Impact of Public Policy: From the Warren Court to the Burger Court and Beyond," *World and I* 1, no. 8 (August 1986): 583.

6. Adler, *We Hold These Truths*, p. 7.

7. Ibid., p. 29. "Here and there" suggests "just a little" or "but not primarily."

8. Ibid.

9. Willmoore Kendall, "Equality: Commitment or Ideal?," *Intercollegiate Review* 24 (Spring 1989): 25–33; also Jack N. Rakove, "On Understanding the Constitution: A Historian's Reflections (and Dissent)," in *Principles of the Constitutional Order: The Ratification Debates*, ed. Robert L. Utley, Jr. (New York: University Press of America, 1989), pp. 33–47.

10. See *The Debates in the Several State Conventions on the Adoption of the Federal Constitution as Recommended by the General Convention at Philadelphia in 1787*, ed. Jonathan Elliot, 5 vols. (New York: J. B. Lippincott, 1876), 4:7–13.

INDEX

Abbot, Henry, 82
Adams, John, 28
Adams, Samuel, 40, 48, 52, 61
Adler, Mortimer, 133–36
American Revolution, 3, 9, 19, 30, 58, 67–68
Ames, Fisher, xvii, 56–58
Annals of Congress, 93, 97
Annapolis Convention, 3
Antifederalists, 34–42
Aristophanes, 7
Aristotle, 6
Articles of Confederation, x, xvi, 3, 12, 17, 20, 27, 31, 34, 36, 42, 54, 63, 68, 74

Backhus, Rev. Isaac, 55
Baldwin, Abraham, 36, 91
Banner, James M., Jr., 44, 55
Barnwell, Robert, 62
Barrell, Nathaniel, 53, 55
Berger, Raoul, 121
Bill of Rights, 13–14, 19, 32, 35, 40, 59, 72, 85, 88, 93–94, 97, 132; incorpo-ration of, 111, 129
Bingham, John A., 114, 118, 123–24
Bloodworth, Timothy, 71, 76, 80, 84
Bonadio, Felice A., 125

Bonham's case, 20
Botein, Stephen, 100
Boudinot, Elias, 91, 98
Bowdoin, James, 28, 48, 51, 53
Boyer, Benjamin M., 123
Bracton, Henry de, 23–30
Bradley, Joseph P., 119
Braxton, Carter, 24
Brearly, David, 91
Brennan, William J., xii, 12
Burke, Aedanus, 98
Burke, Edmund, ix, xix, 21–22
Butler, Pierce, 2, 8, 11, 30, 36, 130
Butterfield, Sir Herbert, 18

Calder v. Bull, 135
Caldwell, Rev. David, 71, 74, 84
Carey, George, 105
Charles I (king of England), 19, 30
Clinton, Sir Henry, 61
Coke, Sir Edward, 20, 30, 120
Congressional Globe, 118, 123
Constitution, British, xx–xxi, 17–33
Constitution, U.S., ix–xiii, xix, 17, 34–41, *et passim*; ratification of, 34–41
Contest over the Ratification of the Federal Constitution in the State of Massachu-setts, The, 43

161